For Laverne Brown, Richard Cloward,
and JoAnn and Allan Widerquist

£13 . 50

Economics for Social Workers

ECONOMICS FOR SOCIAL WORKERS

The Application of Economic Theory to

Social Policy and the Human Services

Michael Anthony Lewis and
Karl Widerquist

COLUMBIA UNIVERSITY PRESS
New York

COLUMBIA UNIVERSITY PRESS
Publishers Since 1893
New York   Chichester, West Sussex

Library of Congress
Cataloging-in-Publication Data

Economics for social workers :
the application of economic theory to
social policy and the human services /
Michael Anthony Lewis and Karl Widerquist.
p. cm.
Includes bibliographical references and index.
ISBN 0–231–11686–1 (cloth : alk. paper)
ISBN 0–231–11687–X (pbk. : alk. paper)
1. Social service—Economic aspects.
2. Economics.
I. Lewis, Michael Anthony, 1965–
II. Widerquist, Karl.
HV41.E24   2002
330'.024'362—dc21   2001047314

Columbia University Press books
are printed on permanent and
durable acid-free paper.

Printed in the United States of America
c 10 9 8 7 6 5 4 3 2 1
p 10 9 8 7 6 5 4 3 2 1

Contents

CONTENTS

Acknowledgments

We would like to thank the following people for reading all or part of this book during its "developmental stages" or for contributing to it in some other manner. First, thanks to John Michel, editor at Columbia University Press, for his support, encouragement, and reading of the entire manuscript. Thanks to Frances Fox Piven, Joel Blau, Jared Bernstein, and Salvatore Brucia for agreeing to read the entire manuscript. A number of doctoral students also read the entire manuscript. Although their consent to do so was a little different from that of the others (since one of the authors made it an assignment), we want to thank them as well. Thanks to Candyce Berger for agreeing to look over our health economics chapter. We would also like to thank Eri Noguchi. Not only did she read part of the manuscript, but she also provided very useful advice about how best to make a point in a way practicing social workers would find accessible. Thanks also to Jessica Godwin for reading part of the manuscript. We would like to thank Gretchen and Miggle Buchenholz for allowing one of us to use the "Hanson Room" during work on this book. Gail Viener was also helpful with the Hanson Room; we would like to thank her as well. Thanks to Ron Harris for his support toward the end of the process. Last, but certainly not least, thanks to Polly Kummel for her excellent copyediting.

Economics for Social Workers

Chapter One

The Economic Perspective

Economics is one of the five main branches of social science, along with sociology, political science, cultural anthropology, and psychology. Social work is considered an applied profession rather than a social science. Social workers are probably more familiar with some of the other branches of social science than with economics, and it might be best to explain the novel by way of the familiar.

All social sciences study aspects of human behavior. One thing humans do is interact with one another to form social systems such as families, groups, organizations, communities, and nation-states. Sociology is the study of social systems. Another thing humans do is act according to systems of shared rules, values, and beliefs, known as cultures and subcultures. Cultural anthropology is the study of cultures and subcultures.[1] Human beings also create formal systems of governance and authority called political systems. Political science is the study of political systems. In addition to creating social systems, behaving in accordance with cultural phenomena, and creating political systems, humans engage in a host of other types of behaviors. For example, they sleep, eat, make love, make war, and become depressed. Psychology studies human behavior in general.

Humans also interact in the marketplace. An oversimplified view of economics would describe it as the study of the marketplace, but economists define their own discipline more broadly. Economics is the study of how humans decide to use available resources to satisfy their wants. Such decisions (whether made in markets, governments, homes, social service agencies, or anywhere else) all fall within the field of economics. In other words, economics is the study of the allocation of scarce resources among competing ends.[2] Stated in this way, the definition of economics probably does not say much to a reader who is new to the field. One reason that understanding what economists say is so difficult is that they often give familiar words technical definitions. We first will define several terms that economists commonly use.

Goods, Resources, Scarcity, and Opportunity Cost

Social workers may not be aware of it, but they produce goods. The economic definition of a **good** is anything that at least one person finds valuable, useful, or desirable. It need not be a physical good; it may also be a service. It need not be traded in the marketplace, either; so long as it is useful to someone, it is a good. Thus, when social workers provide individual counseling, group counseling, and community organizing, they are producing goods, just as automobile workers produce goods when they assemble cars and as professional basketball players produce goods when they entertain audiences.

We find few goods lying around; we need to produce most of them, using other goods. Any goods used in the production of other goods are called **resources,** which are also known as **inputs,** or **factors of production.** Social workers use resources such as their own time and skills, along with physical goods such as computers and office space. Economists usually divide resources into the three broad categories: land, labor, and capital. **Labor** includes not just workers' time but also their knowledge, ability, and skill. These attributes, which make workers more productive, are also known as **human capital**, to emphasize that they are products of past investments, although they still fall under the broad category of labor.[3] Land includes both the land itself and natural resources such as metals, oil, and coal that are taken from the land. The economic definition of *capital* is different from the common definition. Noneconomists often use the term *capital,* or *investment capital,* to mean the money that businesses use to buy the resources they need to facilitate production. According to the economic definition, however, **capital** is material or physical resources used to facilitate production—for example, buildings, machines, paper, and desks. Thus an investor's money is not capital, but some of what it buys is. The money of a social worker who is in private practice is not capital, but the couch on which her clients lie during counseling is. Obviously, if you trace it back far enough, all capital is made up of combinations of natural resources that have been put together by labor in the past. But because capital was in its present state before current production began, it may be best to think of it as a separate factor of production.

Economists define *scarcity* differently from the way it is defined in plain English. Understanding this concept is central to understanding the economic perspective. If you walk into a store and see an aisle filled with nothing but bread, you probably would not consider bread scarce, because in plain English *scarcity* means rare or not plentiful. But from an economic point of view, bread, and anything else you can buy, is scarce. A good is **scarce** if not enough of it is available to put to every conceivable use without sacrificing something else. If more of a good is available than anyone needs or wants, or more of a good can be consumed without sacrificing anything else, that good is **abundant.** If increasing the total amount of consumption of a good requires some sacrifice, that good is scarce.

For example, air is abundant (today). If a child is born, his family will have to sacrifice consumption of some other goods to provide him with food and clothing, but no one will have to sacrifice anything to obtain air for him to breathe. We have more than enough air to go around, even though every person on the planet consumes as much as necessary. When Europeans first colonized the area that became Philadelphia, the Delaware River offered an abundant supply of drinking water. Residents could consume as much as they wanted, and enough remained for everyone else. But thanks to pollution and an increase in population, this is no longer the case; drinking water has become a scarce good nearly everywhere in the United States. In order to consume more water society has to put more resources into sinking wells or building dams or controlling pollution. Land is an example of a scarce good. If more land is used for housing, less is available for social service agencies, shelters for victims of domestic violence, and community centers. More land can be taken for any *one* use but not without making less land available for other uses.

Isn't it true that we are capable of producing more bread than anyone on the planet can eat? Yes, we can but not without sacrificing something else. The land and labor used to produce bread are not available to produce anything else. Dedicating more land to growing wheat means less land on which to build houses, domestic violence shelters, or social service agencies. Dedicating more labor to bake bread means less time to provide social services, build shelters for runaway children, or to stay home and enjoy family life. Every good traded on the market is produced with scarce land, labor, and capital.

Economics is the study of how humans use scarce resources to satisfy competing wants, which are usually assumed to be unlimited. Would you like to have more leisure time than you do now if you could do so without sacrificing something else?[4] Would you like to consume more goods than you do now if you could do so without sacrificing something else? Economists assume that with rare exceptions—such as the very rich—almost everyone would answer yes to both questions. But it is not possible for everyone to have both more leisure time and consume more goods. Consuming more goods means someone must spend more time at work, which means less consumption of leisure time. Therefore, economists conclude that all goods that are bought and sold, no matter how plentiful, are scarce. Abundant goods are free.

Because resources are scarce, agents (individuals, households, social service agencies, firms, governments, etc.) must choose what they most want to attain and allocate resources accordingly. If agents choose to allocate resources to attain one desire, they cannot use those same resources to attain some other desire. In other words, the scarcity constraint means that agents must make trade-offs; economics is, in short, the science of trade-offs. Nonmarket goods, such as love and friendship, arguably can be increased without any trade-off. Such goods are outside the realm of economics, not because economists do not consider them more important than most or all traded goods but because economists study how humans use scarce resources to satisfy their wants. If no trade-off is involved, the economist has no role.

Economists measure trade-offs using the concept of opportunity cost. The **opportunity cost** of a good is the goods forgone in order to obtain that good. For example, a child has been given one dollar. She would like a candy bar and a can of soda, but with that dollar she can buy only one or the other. If she chooses the soda, she has sacrificed one candy bar. Thus the opportunity cost of a can of soda is one candy bar. Or vice versa: the opportunity cost of a candy bar is one can of soda. When a firm invests money in a business, it must take into account not only the money that it invests but also what it would have done with that money had it not invested. Firms could always put money into a stable, safe investment and make, say, 5 percent interest. Thus the opportunity cost of business investments includes not only the money invested but the interest that money could have made in another investment.

The opportunity cost of a government decision is often a little harder to determine. Construction of a battered women's shelter requires the allocation of a given amount of land, labor, and capital. The opportunity cost of the shelter is not the resources needed to produce the shelter, nor is it the money directly used to buy those resources, but the opportunity cost of the shelter depends on what would be produced with those resources if the shelter is not built. The money could be used for a tax cut or to pay off the national debt or to build a CIA training center or many other government projects. If the next best use of the resources is to build the training center, the opportunity cost of one battered women's shelter is one CIA training center. Often the dollar cost of a government project or program is the best available measure of its opportunity cost.

The opportunity cost of a resource allocation decision made by the executive director of a nonprofit social service agency is similar to that made by government. If the director decides to allocate five social workers to providing services in the foster care division, and if the next best use of these social workers' time is counseling residents of the agency's shelter for the homeless, the opportunity cost of allocating these workers to foster care would be the counseling of the homeless that must be forgone. The sum of these social workers' salaries might be the best measure of this opportunity cost.

The Economic Problem

The scarcity of resources means that all human societies must decide how to use the resources available in order to satisfy competing wants. Following the lead of the economics educator Ben Lewis, economists call this "the economic problem."[5] Lewis defined three aspects of this problem: what to produce, how to produce, and for whom to produce. The answers to any one of these questions affect each of the others. A company cannot decide what goods to produce without knowing how those goods will be produced and who will want them, but understanding the differences between these questions is important in order to be able to answer them.

The "what" aspect of the economic problem is the question of what goods society will produce. Societies must decide which desires they most want to satisfy and allocate their resources to the production of the goods that will satisfy those desires. How many cherries will the society produce? How many movies? How many social service agencies, domestic violence shelters, community centers, or homeless shelters will it produce? The "how" aspect is the question of what production methods will be used to produce those goods. What factors of production will the society use? What transportation and energy systems? Will production be more capital intensive or more labor intensive? Will inputs be recycled materials or newly mined natural resources? The "to whom" aspect is the question of who gets to consume the output and in what proportions. On what basis does a person become eligible for a certain amount of consumption? What portion of output goes to wage laborers, parents, retirees, investors, landowners, or the unemployed?

All societies construct social systems called economies, or economic systems, to resolve the economic problem. The two most common ways to address this problem are market exchange or direct government action. An economy in which exchanges between buyers and sellers in markets determine all economic decisions (see chapters 3 and 4) has been called pure capitalism, a pure market economy, a laissez-faire economy, or even a system of natural liberty. An economy in which a government makes all economic decisions has been called a centrally planned economy, a command economy, socialism, or communism. Economies that use both types of decision making are called mixed economies. In practice, pure socialism or pure capitalism do not exist, and all economies are mixed economies. Most capitalist economies require at least some government involvement to define and protect property rights before buyers and sellers can exchange goods. Economies that rely primarily on exchanges between buyers and sellers to allocate resources are called capitalist, although technically they are mixed economies.

The methodology of most economists is first to imagine the workings of a hypothetical pure capitalist system, one of the more common forms of economic systems in the world today, and then examine how government can affect different aspects of such a system. This hypothetical thinking explains why economists tend to talk about "before" and "after" government intervention. Economists use this method to isolate the effects of the two types of decision making.

The market plays a large part in resolving these three questions. Firms largely address the "what" aspect as they decide what to produce by looking at what consumers are willing to pay for and how much they are willing to pay and as consumers decide what to consume by looking at what firms are willing to sell and for what prices. Companies address the "how" aspect as they choose whatever production methods make the largest profit. Customers address the "for whom" aspect as they reward the producers of certain products by purchasing those products.

But the market is not the whole story; the government is involved in all three aspects of the economic problem. The government is both directly and indirectly involved in deciding what goods are produced. Government or government contractors directly produce some goods such as national defense, public hospitals, public schools, and child welfare services. The government prohibits other goods, such as drugs and poisons. The government through its use of selective taxes or tax deductions encourages other goods. For example, allowing people to deduct charitable contributions encourages them to give money to social service agencies, which increases the production of various social services. The government affects the "how" aspect by prescribing some production methods or prohibiting others and also by encouraging research and development with tax breaks and grants to firms and educational institutions.

The government is also heavily involved in the "to whom" aspect. It taxes some individuals and subsidizes others through Social Security, Temporary Assistance for Needy Families (TANF, the program that replaced Aid to Families with Dependent Children following the welfare reforms of 1996), and other programs. It also gives substantial tax breaks to individuals and corporations for a variety of reasons. But perhaps the biggest aspect of government's influence on the "to whom" aspect is easily overlooked. The marketplace rewards individuals not only for what they themselves produce but also for what their property produces. What property people own now depends on what rewards they received in the past, but this in turn depends on what property they owned in the past. If property rights to natural resources are traced far enough, all converge at the point at which a government decided to sell, lend, rent, or give that property to an individual or a firm. Thus the reward for every product sold in a market economy is partially determined by an earlier government decision about who should own the resources with which that product was produced. The paper in this book was produced from trees that the government leased or granted to a paper company. Thus government decisions partially affect all aspects of the economic problem.

Modeling

How and why an architect builds a model of a shopping center or an office complex are easy to see. Less obvious are how and why an economist builds a model of a market. Economists do not generally build physical models, but they build models of a sort. A model is a simplified version of reality that allows an analyst to more easily observe causes and consequences. Economists build logical models of the economy by using assumptions about the structure of markets and the behavior of individuals and institutions. To be useful, a model must be more simple than reality; it is oversimplified only if it misses important features of reality that affect the conclusions that can be derived from the model. Economists are often criticized for the many assumptions of their models. But much of this criticism arises because economists tend to be forthright about specifying their assumptions. Clearly stating the assumptions of a model allows critics to point out exactly where they believe it is weak and to build alternative models that may better represent reality. In this book we will discuss several models of various market structures. Most are based on the assumption of rational behavior.

Rational Behavior

Rational choice theory is a method of modeling human behavior that assumes that agents behave rationally, and the theory is central to the methodology of mainstream economics. An agent is any single economic decision maker—an individual, a household, a firm, a social service agency, or a government official. The word *rational,* in economics, has a different meaning than it has in psychology or in common usage. To a psychologist an individual is rational if his behavior coincides with a set of norms considered healthy. To an economist an agent is rational so long as he has well-defined preferences and behaves consistently with obtaining the most satisfaction he can, given his preferences and the limited resources available to him. It is fair to say that the economic assumption that people are rational is little different than the assumption that people are consistent.

Thus the assumption of rationality is much less restrictive than it sounds to someone who is familiar with the psychological definition of rationality. Many behaviors usually considered pathological are rational in the economic sense. For example, which of these three actors is irrational? Joe spends his entire paycheck the night he gets paid and then starves for the rest of the week. Hannibal kills people and eats them. John rides his car without a seat belt and advocates passage of a law to force him to wear a seat belt. Joe has revealed a strong but rational preference for consumption now rather than consumption later. Hannibal has revealed that he likes eating people so much that he's willing to take the risk that he will be caught and sent to prison; he has also revealed a low amount of sympathy for others. Arguably, both Joe and Hannibal display pathological behavior, but because they behave consistently with *some* set of preferences, no matter how strange those preferences may be, they qualify as economically rational. John, however, by one action reveals a preference for not wearing a seat belt and by another action reveals a preference for wearing one. Only he is behaving irrationally in the economic sense because his actions are contradictory.

The assumption of rational behavior boils down to the assumption that people want to maximize their benefits and minimize costs. Every agent faces a budget constraint. That is, she has only a limited amount of money (or resources) with which to satisfy her material wants. Thus for every desire she satisfies by consuming one thing, she must leave some other desire unsatisfied. A rational agent tries to satisfy as many of her wants as she can with her limited budget. Thus she buys things that have a greater benefit to her than their opportunity cost. For consumers the benefit of buying a material good is called utility. **Utility** is the subjective satisfaction that a consumer experiences from attaining her desires. A good is worth consuming if the utility that it provides is greater than its opportunity cost. Because utility exists only within the psyche of an individual, we can measure it only indirectly, through the economic method of revealed preference.

If Dr. Jones buys a potion for a dollar, he reveals that the potion will be of more use to him than anything else he could have bought with that dollar. He has revealed that the potion provides at least a dollar's worth of utility. If Dr. Smith passes up a potion for a dollar, he has revealed that a potion is not worth a dollar to him at this time. That is, he can buy other things with a dollar that will produce greater utility. Worth, or value (in the utility sense), has nothing to do with what we might call a fair price. No fair or unfair price exists in mainstream economic theory. Utility depends entirely on the use that a consumer receives from a good. The consumer has no control over the price and no knowledge of what the right price is. He simply compares the market price to the utility that he receives from using the item and decides whether to purchase the good.

Economics has three important kinds of agents: households, firms, and government. Households may be either individuals or families. They act as consumers (chapters 2, 3, and 4), laborers (chapter 8), and owners and trustees.[6] As consumers, households decide which goods to purchase by comparing the costs and benefits of each in order to rationally maximize their utility. As laborers, households compare the benefit they receive from work (their wage) to the time they sacrifice to the employer. Economics treats firms, although consumers ultimately own them, as separate entities whose goal is to maximize **profit,** which is the difference between the total revenue they receive from sales and the total cost of the inputs they need to produce the goods they sell. Thus a rational profit-maximizing firm tries to maximize the difference between revenue and costs. Economics uses rational choice theory to study the interaction of firms and households in the marketplace.

Economic models treat government (see chapters 5, 6, and 7) differently. Government does not have a simple goal like maximizing utility, but all the individuals who can affect government decisions have different goals. Thus the same rational choice theory is not as easily applied to government. Sometimes economic models treat the government like an outside force (i.e., if government does X, how will rational households and firms react?). Sometimes government is supposed to have an idea of what is good for society, and the economic model treats government as if it maximizes the benefit to society as a whole. Sometimes the model treats the individual decision makers within government as rational agents out to maximize their own utility or profit, and sometimes the model regards government decisions as the outcome of political interactions of competing interest groups.

Because they are mathematically oriented, economists are typically interested in quantifying benefits and the costs incurred in attaining them. They often do so in terms of money. Imagine that Jack is feeling a little depressed and thinks he might benefit from seeing a social worker. He finds out that the social worker he is considering charges $35 a session. Upon learning this, Jack exclaims, "I am not paying thirty-five dollars a session just to talk to someone!" Jack appears to be saying something about how much he expects that talking with the social worker would benefit him. According to the economic method of revealed preference, Jack does not think the benefit he would receive from talking to a social worker is greater than something else he could buy for $35. Suppose the maximum amount that Jack is willing to pay for a social work session is $25. Economists would say that Jack has revealed that he receives $25 worth of value from talking to a social worker.

Another person may be willing to pay $150 for the same service. Someone else might not be willing to pay even $1. Economists do not ask what this service is "really worth." Any good is worth to an individual whatever she is willing to pay for it. So economists measure benefit or utility by the maximum amount a consumer is willing to pay for a good. Economists measure costs by the amount a consumer actually has to pay to realize his preferences (plus the time and effort to obtain it, costs that may not be easy to measure in dollars and cents).

If Jack is willing to pay $25 for a session with a social worker, this means that he is willing to use this money for counseling instead of to obtain other things that he wants. In other words, Jack is willing to give up or incur an opportunity cost of $25 worth of other goods. For example, suppose Jack likes social work books and could purchase two of them with $25. It follows that Jack is willing to give up two social work books for one counseling session. In other words, the true cost of the social work session is not $25 but the preferences forgone that the $25 represents. If Jack uses $25 to purchase a social work session instead of two social work texts, an economist would say that this reveals that Jack wants one social work session more than he wants two social work books. Note that only the maximum a person is willing to pay for a good reveals the utility he receives from it. Anyone would gladly pay less if he can. However, as chapter 3 shows, the market often forces people to pay the most they are willing for a given good.

Readers might infer that rational choice theory assumes that agents are selfish, because they are concerned with maximizing their own benefits and minimizing their own costs. Indeed, Adam Smith, the eighteenth-century philosopher widely regarded as the founder of modern economics, said, "It is not from the benevolence of the butcher, the brewer or baker, that we expect our dinner, but from their regard to their own self-interest. We address ourselves, not to their humanity but their self-love, and never talk to them of our necessities but of their advantages."[7] It might strike you as unrealistic to assume that all people are selfish, but this assumption carries three qualifications. First, the assumption that people maximize their own utility does not always mean that they are selfish. Although economists generally do assume that people's own satisfaction is all that goes into their utility function, economists do assume that the well-being of others affects one's utility when appropriate. For example, rational models of charitable giving assume that people get utility from knowing that other people are not living in poverty, and rational choice models of parental behavior usually assume that a mother gets utility from knowing that her child is well fed and cared for.[8] Second, in the realm in which economists are usually concerned, selfishness may be the norm. Economics deals mostly with buying and selling in the marketplace. It does not usually deal with the spiritual side of people. When a person goes to the store to buy a tube of toothpaste, it is not unrealistic to think that she has only her own benefit in mind and is not really thinking about what is good for the owner of the store or the workers in the toothpaste-manufacturing plant. Smith, for example, limited his discussion to situations in which a person could benefit without harming another. It is far less cynical to assume this kind of selfishness than to assume that people are willing to harm anyone else to satisfy their own desires. Third, people know a lot about their own preferences and not so much about others'. They may be unaware of how their buying and selling decisions affect others, so they may behave in a manner that can be called selfish, not because they do not care about others but because they do not perceive whether or how their actions affect others.

Microeconomics and Macroeconomics

Economists make a distinction between two broad areas of economics called microeconomics and macroeconomics. Microeconomics is the study of markets for particular goods and services and the differences among economic agents. Which specific goods does a society produce? What affects the distribution of income? What is the price of beans? What is the price of a counseling session with a social worker? Macroeconomics is the study of the economy as a whole, without concern for the different ways that it affects different markets and different people. What is the total output of goods and services in the economy? What is the level of unemployment? What is the inflation rate? This book is mainly, but not exclusively, about microeconomics because this is the area of economics most relevant to analyzing the social welfare issues that social workers are interested in.

Positive Economics and Normative Economics

Another important distinction within the field is between positive and normative economics. Positive economics is concerned with factual issues (what is). Normative economics is concerned with ethical or moral questions (what should be). The statement that "an increase in welfare benefits would cause a decrease in work effort" is a positive statement. It may be either true or false but is not morally right or wrong. The statement that "therefore, we should not increase welfare benefits" is a normative statement. We cannot be judged as true or false but only, depending on our values, as morally right or wrong. Some philosophers might take issue with economists' distinction between positive and normative economics. As they see it, it may be possible for a normative statement like "therefore, we should not increase welfare benefits" to be true or false. Philosophers who hold this point of view are called naturalists and intuitionists.[9] However, these complicated issues are beyond the scope of this book.

This book is mainly about positive economics, but it addresses normative issues as well, because both positive and normative economics are useful for analyzing the policy issues that social workers tend to be interested in. Making a good decision about what a policy should be (normative economics) is impossible without a good idea of its potential effects (positive economics). This book emphasizes positive economics because economists have been more concerned about positive contributions to the field than normative ones.

Economics and Mathematics

Economics, as practiced by modern mainstream economists and many dissenters, is highly mathematical. Those unfamiliar with calculus, matrix algebra, econometrics, set theory, and game theory would have a difficult time understanding most journals in the field. This book contains a more user-friendly approach to economics. Readers do not need a background in complex mathematics to understand this book. An understanding of simple arithmetic and algebra and the ability to read two-dimensional graphs will do, and we keep even this to a minimum. The goal of this book is quite modest: simply to demonstrate the usefulness of economics to social workers by applying some of the most basic economic ideas to issues that interest them, and to help them better understand how economic methodology is used in discussions of U.S. social policy.

Why Social Workers Should Study Economics

Schools of social work in the United States typically require students to take a course in social policy, presumably to provide social workers with tools they need in order to understand how policies affect their clients. Another intention behind the requirement appears to be to provide students with information they need in order to advocate policies that might serve better the needs of clients. A lack of attention to economics prevents these courses from achieving their goals as well as they could.

Economics has exerted considerable influence on how social policy debates in the United States are framed. For example, consider the debate about welfare reform. Welfare reform advocates claim that welfare causes recipients to work less than they would if they were not receiving public assistance, causes families to break up, and causes female recipients to have children to increase their benefits. These views are based on a straightforward application of rational choice theory. Those who do not know rational choice theory cannot adequately respond to these arguments.

A perennial policy debate involves setting the minimum wage. Because minimum wage laws are intended to prevent people from living in poverty, policy-oriented social workers have often supported such laws. Opponents claim that minimum wage laws increase unemployment among unskilled workers—the very group that the laws are largely designed to help. This view is based on an application of the simple economic model of supply and demand. Social workers interested in responding to this view must first understand it.

The dominance of economics in social policy debates means that advocates of policies must demonstrate at least a basic understanding of the economic aspects of their proposals if they want to be considered credible participants.

Chapter Two

Marginal Analysis

Most economists working today are part of the neoclassical school of thought. Other schools of thought in economics include post-Keynesian, institutionalist, Austrian, and Marxist economics. This book focuses on neoclassical economics because it is the mainstream methodology. Other schools will appear in this book as critics of mainstream methods.

Neoclassical economists have used a mathematical approach to modeling human behavior for more than one hundred years. This methodology has often baffled and sometimes enraged critics, but it is as popular now as it has ever been, and a good understanding of it is essential to understanding economics. This methodology allows economists to use mathematics and graphs to predict how people and markets will react to changes in economic conditions, but it involves considerable abstraction from reality.

This methodology is complex, based on assumptions about how an optimal decision is made and how humans behave. This chapter and chapter 3 discuss five parts of the neoclassical method:

The mathematical concepts of the total and the margin
The law of diminishing returns
The marginal method for finding the optimal quantity
The assumption that people actually use the marginalist method
    for determining the optimal quantity
The use of perfect competition as the primary model to study real
    world markets

The first four parts of the neoclassical methodology are the subjects of this chapter; the fifth is the subject of chapter 3. Chapter 4 discusses other models of markets based on similar principles.

To determine a rule for optimal decision making, neoclassical economics uses the concept of the margin, along with the law of diminishing returns. By assuming that individuals actually use the rule, it provides a theory of how consumers and firms behave in markets. By adding additional assumptions about how markets are structured, neoclassical economics builds a theory of how the economy works, which economists use both to determine when a market does or does not produce a socially desirable outcome and to predict how changes in market conditions and the actions of government will affect the economy. Grasping the basic tenets of neoclassical economics will give you a basic understanding of how mainstream economics works, but attaining it requires two chapters of sometimes tedious theories and definitions. Hang in there; it's worth it.

The Total and the Margin

Neoclassical economists' focus on the margin is so central to their methodology that this school of thought was originally known as the marginalist school. The **margin** is the change in the total caused by the last unit. In economics the **total** is always a running total, so every unit is at one point the last unit. The margin becomes important in determining the optimal quantity, but first it must be understood for what it is: a basic mathematical concept.

An example should make it easier to understand the mathematical relationship between the margin and the total. Suppose Bob gets in his car and drives in a straight line away from his home. He drives 60 miles in the first hour, 40 miles in the second hour, and 20 miles in the third hour. Then he stops and does not drive at all in the fourth hour. It is easy to determine the total distance from Bob's home at any time by adding up the distance he traveled in each hour. The marginal distance from Bob's home is simply the amount of distance he traveled in the last unit of time, which in this case is hours but could as easily be minutes or seconds or days or whatever unit is most appropriate. Table 2.1 summarizes the total and marginal distances. At the end of the first hour Bob's total distance from home is 60 miles. His marginal distance is 60 because he added 60 miles to the total in the last hour. At the end of the second hour he is a total of 100 miles from home. His marginal distance is 40. At the end of the third hour the total is 120 and the margin is 20. At the end of the fourth hour he has added no distance to his total, so the total remains at 120 and the margin has fallen to 0. Note that at any point the total is the sum of all the margins up to that point, and the margin is the difference between the current total and the total one unit before.

TABLE 2.1 **Total and Marginal Distance in Bob's Trip**

Unit of Time in Hours	Total Distance	Marginal Distance
1	60	60
2	100	40
3	120	20
4	120	0

What does this have to do with the behavior of consumers and firms in the market? Economists apply these notions of the total and the margin to the variables that enter into firms' and consumers' decision-making processes. Consumers have two things to worry about when they make a purchase—utility and cost. Marginal utility and marginal cost are crucial to consumers' decisions. Firms are concerned with revenue and production cost. Marginal revenue and marginal cost are crucial in firms' decision making.

Total utility is the enjoyment that a consumer gets from all the units of a good that she has consumed thus far. **Marginal utility** is the additional enjoyment of the last unit. The **marginal cost** to a consumer is the price of the good (so long as the price does not vary with the number of units purchased). **Total cost** is the number of units multiplied by the price. **Total revenue** is the amount that a firm receives from all the units that it sells. **Marginal revenue** is the addition to total revenue caused by the last unit (if the price does not vary with the number of units sold, marginal revenue is simply the price). The total cost to a firm is the cost of producing a given amount of output. Marginal cost to a firm is the addition to total cost caused by the last unit.

The Law of Diminishing Returns

The law of diminishing returns is an assumption about the nature of costs and benefits. It states that as the number of units increases, the marginal benefits tend to fall and the marginal costs tend to rise. This law does not state that benefits always fall or that costs always rise (either may rise for any given range of units); it merely states that eventually cost will begin to rise and benefits will begin to fall. If a firm produces more and more of one thing, eventually it will stretch its capacity and the marginal cost will increase. If a consumer consumes more and more of one good, eventually she will reach a satiation point—she does not enjoy additional units as much as she enjoyed earlier units.

For example, suppose the graphs in figure 2.1 show Michael's marginal utility (MU) and total utility (TU) for salty corn chips:

FIGURE 2.1 **Marginal and Total Utility**

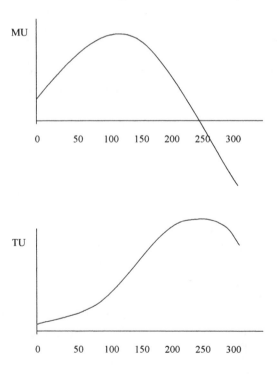

Michael cannot eat just one chip. One chip whets his appetite, and he enjoys the second one even more than the first. He enjoys each chip more than the last until he begins to get full: His enjoyment of each chip begins to decline after he has eaten about one hundred of them. This is the point at which diminishing returns sets in. The marginal utility of each chip declines from then on, but his total utility continues to rise so long as his marginal utility is greater than zero (so long as he got some positive enjoyment out of the last chip, his total utility rises even if he did not enjoy the last chip as much as the previous chip). Total utility rises more slowly after the point of diminishing returns; the higher the marginal utility, the faster total utility rises. Eventually, if he keeps on eating chips, he gets so full that he begins to get a stomachache, and each chip takes away from his enjoyment rather than adding to it; the marginal utility of each chip is less than zero. In Michael's case this happens after he has eaten about 250 chips.

The law of diminishing returns can also be applied to the consumption of counseling. A person who has not received counseling from a social worker obviously would get no subjective satisfaction or total utility from counseling. If each counseling session is considered a unit, the addition to total utility (marginal utility) may increase over the first few. After a certain point the marginal utility of a session may begin to decrease (diminishing returns) and at some point may become negative. For example, suppose a client enters counseling for depression, and a decline in depression is equal to an increase in the total utility of counseling. Over the first few sessions the client's depression may decrease more and more (that is, her marginal utility increases more and more). At some point further sessions may produce smaller decreases in depression (diminishing returns). Eventually, further sessions may actually cause the client to become more depressed (perhaps because an annoying habit of her therapist has become unbearable).

The law of diminishing returns also applies to costs. That is, as you do more and more of something, eventually the marginal cost begins to rise. This is most easily seen from a firm's perspective. Suppose a company has a factory of a given size. If it wants to increase output, it can put more workers in the factory. Eventually, the factory is going to get pretty crowded, and the firm might start using workers at night and on weekends. If a firm has to pay workers time and a half to get them to work the night shift, marginal cost will increase. Eventually, if the firm keeps increasing production, the plant will be full of workers twenty-four hours a day; adding more workers adds little to output, and the cost per unit of output increases.

The Optimal Quantity

The determination of the optimal quantity (given a person's preferences) is a central concept of neoclassical economics. When you think of preferences, you probably think of a simple rank-order, such as I like apples better than oranges and oranges better than toaster ovens and toaster ovens better than unrefined iron ore. But a simple ordering of your favorite goods is not useful to economists interested in building a mathematical model that will predict the quantity of each good that will be sold in a market. People buy various quantities of many products. More important than the question of which good do I like best is the question of how much of each good do I want, given my limited resources. The answer is not simply yes or no but how many. How does a company determine the optimal quantity of each product? How many apples should I buy? 0? 3? 26? 153? How many units should a firm produce? 0? 1? 10? 200? Or 7,584? People can buy an infinite number of combinations of goods. How does a person decide what amount of each good is optimal?

To make this decision, we must start with an objective. Economists believe that the objective in any endeavor can be summed up in one phrase: Maximize the total net benefit. The optimal quantity is the quantity that maximizes the difference between benefits and costs. In consumption benefit is utility. In production benefit is revenue, and net benefit is profit. Thus the complex question of what quantity of each good I should buy from among the infinite number of goods that I could buy can be simplified to a basic question. Start with one unit of one good. Is the marginal benefit greater than the marginal cost of that good? If the benefit is greater than the cost, buy it. If the benefit is greater than the cost, it has a positive net benefit; it adds more to total utility than it does to total cost. Repeat this procedure for the second unit. Keep on repeating it for as long as the marginal benefit exceeds the marginal cost. Eventually, the law of diminishing returns will come into play, and either the benefits will fall or the costs will rise until the marginal cost equals the marginal benefit. Stop—that's the optimal quantity. When the marginal benefit is just equal to the marginal cost, you are indifferent to purchasing the last unit. That also means that you have gotten every last bit of net benefit out of this consumption that you can.

A concise way to state this whole procedure is that the optimal quantity is the point at which the marginal cost equals the marginal benefit. At that point the total net benefit (the sum of all the marginal benefits of each unit minus the marginal costs of each unit) is maximized. Economists typically use mathematical equations to represent costs and benefits and calculus to determine the optimal quantity. This book spares you all that and illustrates it with figure 2.2.

FIGURE 2.2 **The Optimal Quantity**

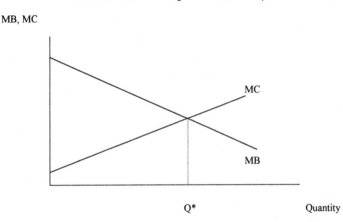

Marginal benefit (MB) starts high and falls, and marginal cost (MC) starts small and rises. Each unit smaller than Q^* (to the left of Q^* on the graph) has benefits greater than cost and thus adds to the total net benefit. Each unit to the right of Q^* has a negative net benefit. Consuming the amount Q^*, then, takes advantage of all the net gains possible. Keep in mind that costs are, as always, measured in opportunity cost. The cost is not simply the money cost but the utility that that money could generate if it were used to purchase any other good. Therefore, if the benefit is higher than the cost, buying this good is more worthwhile than using this amount of money to buy any other good.

This method can be used for any type of decision making. How many workers should a firm hire? It should hire that quantity at which the marginal benefit of the last worker (measured by what he produces) is equal to his marginal cost (his wage). How much money should the government spend on the production of homeless shelters? It should spend the amount at which the marginal cost of an additional shelter equals the marginal benefit. How many counseling sessions should a client purchase? She should keep purchasing sessions until the marginal benefit of a session equals the marginal cost. How many cookies should an economist eat? He should eat the amount at which the marginal utility of the last cookie equals its marginal cost.

But how can you measure the marginal utility of a cookie (or any other consumer product)? We can do this by using the opportunity cost principle outlined in chapter 1. The marginal cost of a cookie, in the opportunity cost sense, is quite simple: It is the price. The price represents the amount of other goods a consumer must give up in order to buy one cookie. If a cookie costs $1, then for every cookie I eat, I have one less dollar to spend on all other goods. The marginal benefit of a cookie is a little bit trickier. You have to ask yourself how much you would pay for this cookie. What would be the *most* I would give up for this cookie if I had to? Suppose you eat one cookie and it tastes so good that you would be willing to sacrifice $4 worth of other goods to buy it. That's your marginal utility. Luckily, you had to pay only $1, so it was a good deal for you. So have another. Now that you have already had a cookie, the second one is not nearly so satisfying, but it is still good—so you would pay $2 for it. Still a good deal. Now that you are becoming satisfied, the third cookie is only worth $1 to you. It costs $1, so it is worth it but just barely. You are indifferent to this third unit. That is how you know you have reached the optimum, and it is time to stop eating cookies. If you apply this principle to all goods that you purchase, you will be indifferent to the last unit of each good that you consume.

The Assumption of Rational Self-Interested Behavior

In practice the assumption that agents are rational, discussed in chapter 1, means that people actually make decisions by comparing the marginal cost and marginal benefits to determine the optimal quantity. It is one thing to say that the marginal method will determine the optimal quantity, but it is quite another to say that people actually behave that way. Yet this is just what the assumption of rational self-interested behavior states. Neoclassical economists treat consumers and producers as if they were little calculating machines who have a given set of goals and behave consistently with those goals, using the rules of optimal decision making to make choices. Even if you have never heard the term *marginal utility* before, neoclassical economists believe that you behave as if you have been using it all your life to determine how much of each good to buy. The reason for the assumption that people act rationally is that it allows economists to build economic models in which people behave predictably. This predictability allows economists to use mathematical equations and graphs to describe peoples' preferences and to predict how people will respond to changes in prices and market conditions.

The assumption that people follow the optimal decision-making rule reveals more information about the example from the last chapter. Chapter 1 said that the amount of utility that Jack would obtain from seeing a social worker is measured by how much he would be willing to pay for it and that he must value the good at least as much as its price ($25) or he would not purchase it. If Jack is willing to pay a maximum of $25 (give up a maximum of $25 worth of other goods) for a social work session, $25 is the marginal utility of this session. If his marginal utility was so high that he would pay $150 for a session, he would purchase a large number of sessions until his marginal utility fell to $25. If Jack's marginal utility was less than $25, he would not purchase any sessions. Using the theory of rational behavior, and the optimal decision-making rule, the price reveals a lot of information about consumer preferences. All consumers who purchase the good receive a marginal utility of exactly $25 from the last unit that they purchased (although the marginal utility for earlier quantities might be much higher); all consumers who do not purchase it value the good at less than $25.

While consumers maximize utility, firms maximize profit. Profit, also known as rent, is defined differently in economics than in ordinary English, so economics sometimes refers to economic profit, or economic rent. In ordinary English profit is the rate of return on investment: If you invest $100 and you make $104, you have made a profit of 4 percent. But an economist defines *profit* in an opportunity cost sense. If you invest $100 in industry A, you have profited only if you make more than you could have if you had put that money into another investment. Suppose that the normal rate of return is 2 percent. The opportunity cost of investing $100 in industry A is $102. If the investment returns less than $102, the investor wishes he had not invested in that industry. If the investment pays exactly $102, the investor is indifferent—this investment is the same as any other normal investment. Any return greater than $102 is profit. Thus the economic profit of an investment that returns $104 is only 2 percent.

The reason the term *profit,* or *rent,* is important is that any return equal to or greater than the normal rate of return is sufficient to keep investing in this industry; anything more than the normal rate of return is just gravy for the investor. Rent does not apply only to firms; it can also apply to any return greater than what is needed to keep a resource in its present employment. For example, suppose Jay is a social worker who earns $40,000 a year. Jay would be willing to remain in his current job for any salary that is at least $30,000 a year. Jay receives an economic rent of $10,000 a year.

Keynesian (or post-Keynesian) economists, who stress the economics of uncertainty, often break with neoclassical economists over the assumption of rational utility- (or profit-) maximizing behavior. They may agree that equating marginal cost and benefit would determine the optimal quantity if the correct information were available, but often it is not. People might not know all the costs and benefits that they would receive from consuming any given quantity of any given good, so they have to guess. Firms face even more barriers to rational behavior. They would need to know exactly how many goods consumers want to buy and exactly what they would pay for those goods in order to rationally determine the optimal quantity of goods to produce and of workers to hire. Keynesians stress that firms cannot know this information and so will have to guess and will often guess wrong. Keynesians believe that uncertainty will make it nearly impossible for consumers and firms to determine the optimal quantity and that recessions and depressions will result.

Not every critic of neoclassical economics criticizes the rational decision-making assumption. But nearly every critic of neoclassical economics has some objection to the perfectly competitive model of the marketplace. Although neoclassical economics has several other models of market structure (discussed in chapter 4), perfect competition is the neoclassical economist's primary model for studying the economy. The next chapter describes how it works and how it is used before discussing common criticisms of it.

Chapter Three

Perfect Competition and the
Supply-and-Demand Model

In economic theory a **market** is a place where buyers and sellers come together to make exchanges. The boundaries of a market depend on the good in question. For two sellers to be considered part of the same market, they must be close enough so consumers could reasonably view the two as substitutes. For example, the corner supermarket is not a market in the economic sense. The local market for groceries consists of all the grocery transactions in a neighborhood, but it would not include a store across town if consumers believed it was too far away from them to use. But the housing market may extend across a city or a metropolitan area. A market is not necessarily a physical space. For example, Internet travel agencies are a market that potentially stretches around the entire world. Economists have several different models they use to study various kinds of markets, and they focus most of their attention on one particular type called perfect competition.

The Assumptions of the Perfectly Competitive Model

Perfect competition (or competition, for short) is a theory of how some markets operate. It is a highly simplified (and some would say idealized) theory. Economists use it both to predict how market prices and quantities react to changes in market conditions and to demonstrate the efficiency of the market system. The following conditions must hold for a market to be perfectly competitive:

1. *Small buyers and sellers.* The market has many buyers and sellers, all of whom are too small relative to the size of the market for the behavior of any one to affect the market price; any firm or consumer can sell or buy all it wants without affecting the market price.
2. *Homogeneous product.* The goods sold by one firm in the market are identical to the goods sold by any other firm in the market.
3. *Perfect information.* All buyers and sellers know everything there is to know about quality, prices, locations, and any other relevant factors that may affect their decision to buy or sell goods in the market.
4. *Free entry and exit.* The market has no barriers that would prevent buyers and sellers from entering or exiting at will.

Not many markets in the real world meet these conditions, but that does not mean that the model of perfect competition is useless. A good understanding of the perfectly competitive model is necessary for at least four reasons. First, some actual markets approximate perfect competition, such as stock markets and farming. Second, even markets that are further from the perfectly competitive model, such as the housing market, may be similar enough to make the theory useful in understanding how that market works. Third, as discussed shortly, the absence of any one of these conditions is a standard justification for government intervention. Fourth, the perfectly competitive model is so widely used to examine the effects of economic policy that anyone who hopes to understand policy debates must understand it.

The rest of this chapter demonstrates that if the four assumptions of the perfectly competitive model hold, three important conclusions follow. First, all transactions in the market take place at the same price, and all buyers and sellers take the market price as given. Second, the interaction of supply and demand impersonally determines the market price and quantity. Third, the equilibrium quantity is socially optimal (which we will define shortly).

The conclusion that all buyers and sellers take the market price as given follows from the first three assumptions. Firms cannot use tactics like restricting their output to achieve a higher price because they are small relative to the size of the market. If a firm charges a price higher than the market price, consumers will simply buy it from one of the many other sellers in the market, and the firm will lose all its sales. Perfectly competitive companies cannot use a claim of high quality to obtain a higher price because perfectly informed consumers know that all firms sell an identical product. Firms have no incentive to sell below the going rate because they are small in relation to the size of the market. No profit-maximizing firm that can sell all it wants at the going price would ever sell it for a lower price; that would just be turning away money. For similar reasons consumers must also take the market price as given.

Although individual firms and consumers have no control over the price of the good, they have complete control over the quantity they want to exchange. Consumers ask themselves, given the market price, what quantity should I buy to maximize my utility? Companies ask themselves, given the market price what quantity should I sell to maximize my profit? If firms do not set the price and consumers do not set the price, who or what does? In a perfectly competitive market the interaction of supply and demand sets the price.

Demand

Demand is the relationship between the price and the quantity that consumers are willing to buy, all else being equal. This relationship must be defined for a given market over a given period of time. The phrase "all else being equal" means that price is the only factor that can change—any other factors that may affect the quantity that consumers are willing to buy remain static. If they do change, the relationship between price and the amount consumers are willing to buy will also change. Consumers' willingness to buy must mean that they actually will buy it, given their income and other factors. The amount that consumers would be willing to buy if they had more money is not relevant to the determination of market price and quantity and is best left out of the discussion.

Demand, then, is the entire relationship between all prices and the quantity that consumers are willing to buy at those prices. The quantity that consumers are willing to buy is called the **quantity**

demanded. Although the terms *demand* and *quantity demanded* sound similar, the distinction between them is extremely important: quantity demanded is one quantity at one given price; demand is the entire relationship between all quantities demanded and all possible prices.

Generally, the relationship between price and the quantity demanded is inverse, or negative. That is, when the price goes up, the quantity demanded goes down, and when the price goes down, the quantity demanded goes up. This general relationship is called the *law of demand*. This relationship exists for two main reasons. First, when a good becomes less expensive, people who are already buying it have an incentive to buy more; people who previously were not buying it may decide to start buying it. Second, when the price increases, some people may buy less and others may stop buying it altogether. It is possible that some consumers will buy the same amount when price changes slightly, but if enough consumers in the market change their behavior because of the price change, the law of demand will still hold for the market as a whole.

Economists use the word *law* a lot, and perhaps they exaggerate a bit. The word *law* implies that the principle is true at all times and all places, like the law of gravity. But economic laws are not as strict as the laws of physics; they all have exceptions. Economists believe that price and the quantity demanded generally tend to be negatively related, but this law might not hold for some goods at some given range of prices. For example, if the price of insulin doubles, diabetics may still buy the same amount. Or certain goods that have snob appeal may be more attractive to consumers if they cost more. However, economists generally believe these exceptions are rare. And of course some price is so high that even a critically ill person will not be able to afford expensive medication and even a snobby millionaire cannot afford to go to the moon as a tourist.

Demand can be represented mathematically, graphically, or in the form of a table. The graphic representation of demand is called the demand curve. The representation of demand in the form of a table is called a demand schedule. The mathematical representation of demand is called a demand function. All these representations are tools to help us better use and understand the concept of demand. The focus of this book is an understanding of the concepts; it uses graphs and tables to aid this understanding, but it keeps them to a minimum and leaves mathematics to more advanced textbooks.

Table 3.1 shows a hypothetical demand schedule for rental housing in Metropolis.

TABLE 3.1 **Market Demand for Rental Housing**

Price (MONTHLY RENT)	Quantity (UNITS PER MONTH)
$450	2 million
$350	4 million
$250	6 million
$150	8 million
$50	10 million

Price in the rental market is called rent, but the word *rent* is also used for the act of buying or selling a rental unit. In plain English you would not say that you bought a rental item; you would say, "I didn't buy it, I rented it." But in economics *renting* is defined differently: The good purchased is not the apartment but the use of an apartment for one month. At a price of $450 a month consumers are willing to rent 2 million units. At a price of $350 they are willing to rent 4 million units. At a price of $250 they are willing to rent 6 million units, and so on. In accordance with the law of demand, consumers buy more at lower prices and less at higher prices.

Figure 3.1 shows the demand curve for the same rental housing market. The downward slope of the curve (from left to right) illustrates the law of demand. A demand curve gives a more complete picture of demand. Remember that demand relates all possible prices to the quantities demanded at those prices. A table can show only a few representative prices and quantities, whereas a graph can show many more. The demand curve is read by finding the price on the vertical axis, looking straight across to the demand curve, and then straight down to the horizontal axis.

Elasticity of Demand

The **price elasticity of demand,** also called the **elasticity of demand,** is a measure of the sensitivity to price of the quantity demanded. It is often not enough to say that the quantity decreases when the price increases,

FIGURE 3.1 **Market Demand Curve for Rental Housing**

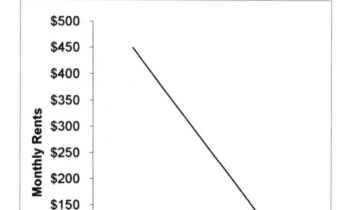

but it is important to measure how much quantity responds to changes in price. Businesses want to know whether an increase in their price will cause a major decline in sales. Policymakers want to know whether a sales tax will significantly affect the local economy. Economics uses elasticity of demand to measure such effects in percentage terms: the percentage change in quantity demanded for a given percentage change in price. We have a formula for calculating price elasticity of demand, but we will spare readers the burden of having to learn it. The importance of measuring sensitivity of demand in percentage terms is that the resulting number does not depend on the units in which the prices and quantities are measured. Whether the good is measured in pounds, tons, meters, gallons, hours, or anything else has no effect on how its elasticity is measured because the resulting figure is a ratio. Thus elasticity allows us to compare the sensitivity of demand in any market to the sensitivity in any other.

If the elasticity of demand is greater than 1, the percentage change in quantity is larger than the percentage change in price. That is, the quantity demanded is rather sensitive to price changes. If elasticity of demand is greater than 1, demand is elastic. If the elasticity of demand is less than 1, the percentage change in quantity is smaller than the percentage change in price. That is, the quantity demanded is relatively insensitive to price. This is not to say that demand is completely insensitive to price; increases in price still cause decreases in the quantity demanded, but that decrease in demand is smaller (in percentage terms) than the increase in price. If the elasticity of demand is zero, demand is completely insensitive to price, and consumers purchase the same amount regardless of price.

For example, if the price elasticity of demand for health care were 0.5, and the price of health care increased by 10 percent, the quantity of health care demanded would fall by only 5 percent. The demand for health care is inelastic, because the percentage change in the quantity demanded was smaller than the percentage change in price. If the price elasticity of theater tickets were 2, a 10 percent decrease in the price of theater tickets would cause a 20 percent increase in the number of tickets sold. The demand for theater tickets is elastic, because the percentage change in the quantity demanded was larger than the percentage change in price. Note that even though the law of demand holds in both cases (the quantity demanded goes up when the price goes down and vice versa), the sensitivity of demand to price is quite different.

Price elasticity of demand is also useful for social policy analysis. Suppose Congress enacts a cigarette tax to discourage smoking. However, some economists have found empirical evidence that the demand for cigarettes is very inelastic, so a substantial increase in price will have little effect on smoking. This could be because smokers are addicts who find it very painful to reduce their cigarette consumption. If so, increased taxes would not be very effective at reducing the number of smokers, although it may be useful to raise revenue, which can be used to hire social workers to discourage people from smoking and also pay the increased medical cost of smokers. Some studies have shown that although the demand for cigarettes is inelastic in the short run, high prices discourage people from starting to smoke and so may have a substantial long-term effect on smoking.

Supply

Supply is the relationship between the price and the quantity that firms are willing to sell, all else being equal. As with demand, this relationship must be defined for a given market over a given period of time. Companies' willingness to sell must mean that they actually will sell the item, given their cost of production and other factors. Like demand, supply is the entire relationship between all prices and the quantity that firms are willing to sell at those prices. The quantity that sellers are willing to sell is called the **quantity supplied.** Quantity supplied is one quantity at one given price; supply is the entire relationship between all the quantities supplied and all possible prices.

Generally, the relationship between price and the quantity supplied is positive. That is, when the price goes up, the quantity supplied goes up, and when the price goes down, the quantity supplied goes down. This general relationship is called the law of supply. This relationship holds because when the market price of a good increases, it becomes more profitable to sell that good, giving companies an incentive to put more resources into producing and selling that good rather than other goods. Like demand, supply can be represented mathematically, graphically, or in the form of a table. The graphic representation of supply is called the supply curve. The representation of supply in the form of a table is called a supply schedule. The mathematical representation of supply is called a supply function.

Table 3.2 shows a hypothetical supply schedule for rental housing in Metropolis.

Landlords offer 10 million units at a price of $450 a month. They offer 8 million at a price of $350. They offer 6 million units at a price of $250

TABLE 3.2 Market Supply for Rental Housing

Price (MONTHLY RENT)	Quantity (UNITS PER MONTH)
$450	10 million
$350	8 million
$250	6 million
$150	4 million
$50	2 million

FIGURE 3.2 Market Supply Curve for Rental Housing

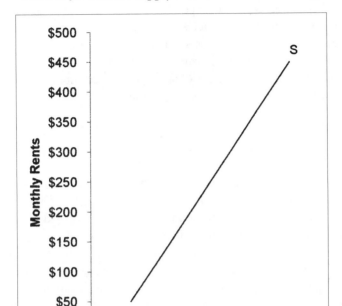

and so on. In accordance with the law of supply, firms are willing to offer more for sale at higher prices and fewer at lower prices. Figure 3.2 shows the supply curve for the same rental housing market. The upward slope of the curve (from left to right) illustrates the law of supply. The supply curve is read by finding the price on the vertical axis, looking straight across to the supply curve, and then straight down to the horizontal axis to find the quantity supplied that goes with that price.

Elasticity of Supply

Price elasticity of supply, also called **elasticity of supply,** is a measure of the sensitivity to price of the quantity supplied. If the elasticity of supply is greater than 1, the percentage change in quantity supplied will be larger than the percentage change in price. That is, the quantity supplied is rather sensitive to price changes. If elasticity of supply is greater than 1, supply is elastic. If the elasticity of supply is less than 1, the percentage change in quantity supplied is smaller than the percentage change in price. That is, the quantity demanded is relatively insensitive to price. If the price elasticity of the supply of bread is 2, a 1 percent increase in price causes a 2 percent increase in quantity supplied.

Equilibrium

The **equilibrium price** in a perfectly competitive market is determined by the intersection of supply and demand—the one point at which the quantity demanded equals the quantity supplied. It is called the equilibrium because at that price there is no tendency to change, and at any other price there is a tendency for the price to change to the equilibrium price. At any price higher than the equilibrium price, the quantity supplied is greater than the quantity demanded; firms cannot sell all they want at the going price, creating pressure for the price to fall until it reaches equilibrium. At any price less than the equilibrium, the quantity demanded is greater than the quantity supplied; consumers cannot buy all they want at the going price, creating pressure for the price to rise until it reaches equilibrium. At the equilibrium, quantity demanded equals the quantity supplied, and pressure for the price to change does not exist. The **equilibrium quantity** corresponds to the equilibrium price and is the point at which quantity demanded and quantity supplied are equal.

TABLE 3.3 **Equilibrium in the Rental Housing Market**

Price (MONTHLY RENT)	Quantity Demanded (UNITS PER MONTH)	Quantity Supplied (UNITS PER MONTH)
$450	2 million	10 million
$350	4 million	8 million
$250	6 million	6 million
$150	8 million	4 million
$50	10 million	2 million

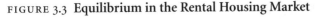

FIGURE 3.3 **Equilibrium in the Rental Housing Market**

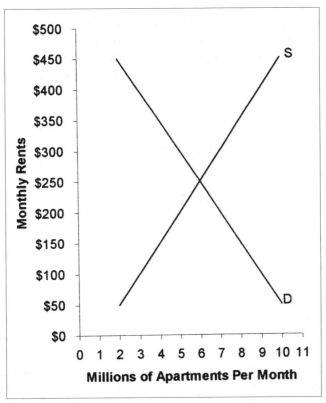

Table 3.3 and figure 3.3 illustrate equilibrium in the housing market in Metropolis.

At a price of $250 a month quantity demanded and quantity supplied are both 6 million units. This is the equilibrium. At a price of $450 a month consumers demand only 2 million dwellings, while landlords are willing to supply 10 million. Landlords cannot sell all they want, so they have an incentive to lower their price. A lower price would lead to an increase in the quantity demanded and a decrease in the quantity supplied, reducing the pressure for prices to fall, but the pressure for prices to fall would not be eliminated until the price reached equilibrium. At a price of $50 a month consumers demand 10 million dwellings, but landlords are willing to supply only 2 million. Consumers cannot buy all they want at the market price, so they have an incentive to bid the price up until it reaches equilibrium.

Only at equilibrium can both consumers purchase all they want and firms sell all they want at the going price, so no one has an incentive to change behavior. Only at a price of $250 a month is there no pressure for the price of rental housing to change. In other words, the $250 price is the one at which the market stabilizes. Consumers will exchange their money for the 6 million dwellings, and both they and the landlords with whom they have done business will be satisfied. This does not mean that everyone is happy. Consumers would rather buy more at a lower price, but firms will not go along; firms would rather sell more at a higher price, but consumers will not go along. Equilibrium is simply a point at which the behavior of firms matches the behavior of consumers.

The vertical axis of figure 3.3 displays price, while the horizontal axis displays quantity. This graph is another way to present the information in table 3.3. The demand and supply curves intersect where the price is $250 and quantity is 6 million units, the equilibrium price and quantity. Note that at prices higher than $250, quantity demanded is less than the quantity supplied, and at prices lower than $250 the quantity demanded is greater than the quantity supplied. Graphic displays of supply and demand are useful because they permit a clear depiction of what happens when supply and demand change.

Free entry and exit ensure that economic profit (also known as economic rent) will be zero at equilibrium in a perfectly competitive market. Remember that economic profit is a return greater than the normal rate of return. Therefore, saying that there are no profits does not mean that companies are not making money; it simply means that they are not making any more money than they would if they invested their money in their next best option. Thus, saying that there are no economic profits just means that the rate of return equalizes across all industries that have free entry and exit. If there are profits in one market, companies recognize that they can make more money in this market than other markets and enter the market until those profits disappear. If there are negative profits, companies recognize that they can do better in other markets and exit the market until a normal rate of return is reestablished. The zero economic profit equilibrium is a long-run condition. It takes time for companies to react to profit possibilities in other industries; for however long that takes, positive economic profits can exist in perfectly competitive industries.

Changes in Demand

Demand remains stable only so long as all other factors that affect demand do not change. Other factors can either increase or decrease the entire demand relationship. An increase in demand means that at any given price consumers are willing to buy more than before. As figure 3.4 shows, the entire demand curve shifts to the right, showing that at any particular price consumers will buy more. A decrease in demand means that at any given price consumers are willing to buy less than they did before. Figure 3.5 illustrates a decrease in demand. The factors that can cause a change in demand are consumers' preferences, consumers' income, the prices of other goods, the size of the population, and climate.

PREFERENCES. Most economists consider consumers' preferences to be outside their realm of study. Consumers occasionally change their preferences for whatever reason. If consumers decide they like a good

FIGURE 3.4 **Increase in Demand**
The demand shifts to the right from the original demand curve (D_1) to the new demand curve (D_2), showing that at any given price consumers are willing to buy more. The equilibrium price increases from P_1 to P_2, and the equilibrium quantity increases from Q_1 to Q_2.

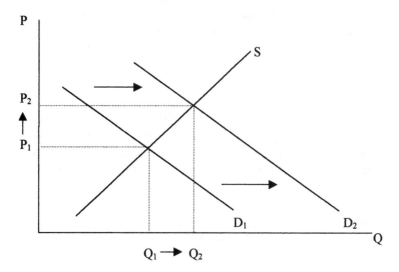

FIGURE 3.5 **Decrease in Demand**
The demand shifts to the left from the original demand curve (D_1) to the new demand curve (D_2), showing that at any given price consumers are willing to buy less. The equilibrium price decreases from P_1 to P_2, and the equilibrium quantity decreases from Q_1 to Q_2.

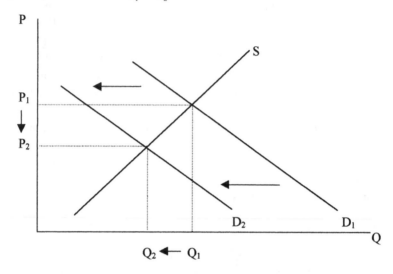

more than they used to, demand will increase; if they find that they do not like it as much as before, demand will decrease. For example, if consumers become worried about the health effects of smoking, they may decide they are not willing to purchase as many cigarettes as before.

INCOME. A change in consumers' incomes will affect not only how many goods a consumer can afford but often also the types of goods that consumers buy. As consumers' incomes rise, they will demand more of most goods; goods for which this is the case are called **normal goods**, or **superior goods**. Demand for some goods, called **inferior goods**, decreases when incomes increase; typically, these are goods that people buy when they cannot afford other, more desirable goods. For example, suppose Hamburger Hash is an inferior good and filet mignon is a normal good. If consumers' incomes rise, their demand for filet mignon will increase, and their demand for Hamburger Hash will decrease.

PRICE OF RELATED GOODS. Prices of other goods and services can affect demand in two different ways. **Complements** are goods that are used together. An increase in the price of one complement decreases the demand for the other. For example, if the price of chips increases, demand for dip will decrease, because people will eat fewer chips with dip. **Substitutes** are goods that can be used in place of one another. If the price of one increases, the demand for the other increases. For example, if the price of tea increases, the demand for coffee will increase, because people will be looking for something hot to drink besides tea.

CLIMATE. Weather can strongly affect demand for some goods. Demand for air conditioners is higher during hot summers than cool ones. Global warming will cause the demand for air conditioners to increase and the demand for snow shovels to decrease.

POPULATION. The more consumers live in a given area, the more demand there will be for goods sold in that area. Changes in population may affect some goods more than others, but in general an increase in the population increases demand for all goods.

Changes in Supply

Like demand, supply remains stable only so long as all other factors that affect supply do not change. Other factors can increase or decrease the entire supply relationship. An increase in supply means that at any given price firms are willing to sell more than before. The entire supply curve shifts to the right, showing that at any particular price firms are willing to sell more. A decrease in supply means that, at any given price, companies are willing to sell less than before. Figure 3.6 illustrates an increase in supply, and figure 3.7 shows a decrease in supply. These graphs may be a little confusing because when supply increases, the curve does not go up—it goes out, and when supply decreases, it does not move down—it moves in. This happens because an increase in supply means that for any given price firms are willing to sell more, and a decrease means that at any given price firms are willing to sell less. If you compare the second supply curve in figure 3.7 with the first supply curve, you will see that the quantity demanded at any given price is less after the shift than before. Several factors can cause shifts in supply, including the size of the industry, changes in technology, prices of inputs, and the prices of related outputs.

THE SIZE OF THE INDUSTRY. An increase in the size of the industry, that is, an increase in the number of companies in the industry, causes the supply to increase. The larger the number of firms in an industry, the larger will be the quantity supplied at any given price. The smaller the number of firms, the smaller the quantity supplied.

TECHNOLOGY. A change in technology shifts the supply curve. If some technological development allows firms to produce more goods from a given amount of inputs, they will be able to increase output at any given price, and the supply curve will shift to the right (increase).

THE PRICE OF INPUTS. Inputs (or resources) also affect supply. If a firm has to pay more for workers, rent, or raw materials, it reduces the quantity of the good supplied at any given price. In other words, it will need a higher price in order to sell the same level of output.

PRICES OF RELATED OUTPUTS. The price of other outputs can affect supply in two different ways. Substitute outputs are goods that can be produced using the same resources, and firms must decide whether to produce one or the other. For example, dairy farmers can sell cheese or milk from the same cow. If cheese prices rise, farmers will sell more cheese, thereby reducing the supply of milk. Outputs can also be by-products of each other. For example, beef and leather are both made from dead cattle. If the price of beef falls, farmers will raise fewer cattle and the supply of leather will decrease.

The Effects of Changes in Supply and Demand on Equilibrium Price and Quantity

One of the most important uses of supply and demand is to predict how equilibrium price and quantity will respond to changes in the market. The method is very simple: For any given change, figure out whether it affects supply or demand, figure out whether it is an increase or decrease, draw the shift on a supply-and-demand graph, and observe what happens to equilibrium price and quantity. The four graphs that follow are the most important graphs in this book. We will refer to them through-out the remaining chapters. Even if you understand nothing else in this book, you will still have learned something significant about how economic theory works.

Figure 3.4 illustrates an increase in demand. The entire demand curve shifts to the right. The equilibrium price and quantity both increase. Supply (the supply curve) does not change, but the quantity supplied does. It increases as the equilibrium point moves along the supply curve. Thus mainstream theory predicts that anything that causes demand to increase will cause the equilibrium price and quantity to increase. How much price and quantity change depends on the elasticity of supply. The more elastic the supply curve (geometrically, the closer the supply curve is to being completely horizontal), the more an increase in demand will cause the quantity to increase; the less elastic or more inelastic the supply curve is (geometrically, the closer the supply curve is to being completely vertical), the more price will increase.

Figure 3.5 illustrates a decrease in demand. The demand curve shifts to the left, showing that at any given price consumers will buy less than before. The equilibrium price and quantity both decrease. Again, supply does not change, but the quantity supplied decreases. Thus the theory predicts that anything that causes demand to decrease will cause a decrease in both price and quantity.

Figure 3.6 illustrates an increase in supply. The supply curve shifts out (to the right), showing that at any given price firms are willing to sell less. The equilibrium price decreases, and the equilibrium quantity increases. How much price and quantity change depends on the elasticity of demand. The more elastic demand is (the closer the demand curve is to being completely horizontal), the bigger the effect will be on quantity and the less the effect will be on price. The less elastic or more inelastic demand is (the closer the demand curve is to being completely vertical), the bigger the effect will be on price and the smaller the effect will be on quantity.

Figure 3.7 illustrates a decrease in supply. The supply curve shifts in (to the left), showing that at any given price companies are willing to sell less than before. When the supply curve shifts to the left, the equilibrium price increases and the quantity decreases. The more elastic demand is, the more quantity will decrease and the less price will increase; the less elastic demand is, the more price will increase and the less quantity will decrease.

FIGURE 3.6 **Increase in Supply**

The supply curve shifts to the right from the original supply curve (S_1) to the new supply curve (S_2), showing that at any given price firms are willing to sell more. The equilibrium price decreases from P_1 to P_2, and the equilibrium quantity increases from Q_1 to Q_2.

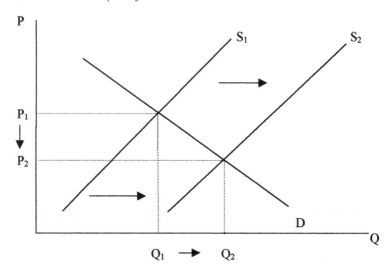

Note that when demand changes, price and quantity move in the same direction, but when supply changes, price and quantity move in opposite directions. This is because when demand increases, when consumers want to buy more, they have to offer firms a higher price to encourage them to produce more. When supply increases, when firms want to sell more, they have to offer consumers a lower price to encourage them to buy more.

You can use supply and demand as a tool to help you examine the effects of changes in the market. For example, how would the apple market be affected if a hurricane knocked down half the orange trees in Florida? This would lead to a decrease in the number of firms producing oranges, or a shift to the left of the supply curve as shown in figure 3.7. Reading from that figure, the price of oranges would increase, and the quantity would decrease. Thus people are buying fewer oranges. Apples are a substitute for oranges, so the demand for apples will increase (see fig. 3.4). Reading from that figure, the equilibrium quantity of apples will

FIGURE 3.7 **Decrease in Supply**
The supply curve shifts to the left from the original supply curve (S_1) to the new supply curve (S_2), showing that at any given price firms are willing to sell fewer goods. The equilibrium price increases from P_1 to P_2, and the equilibrium quantity decreases from Q_1 to Q_2.

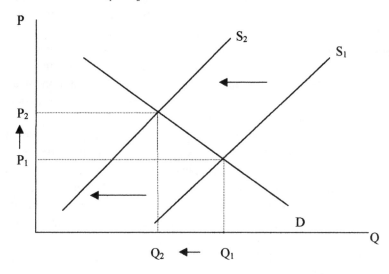

increase, as will the equilibrium price. This is how supply and demand are used to predict changes in markets.

Efficiency in the Perfectly Competitive Market

In 1776 Adam Smith first proposed the idea that the entire society benefits from exchanges made by selfish individuals in competitive markets. In his book, *The Wealth of Nations,* Smith called this theory the invisible hand.[1] It has been extended and codified by economists since Smith and is now called the first fundamental theorem of welfare economics.[2] Smith proposed that if all trade is purely voluntary (there is no theft, fraud, or coercion, and there are no disruptions in the marketplace), if trade is not restricted, if all people trade for their own interests, and if there is a given distribution of property rights, the market will produce a result that is beneficial to all and even maximally beneficial. This is so because Smith has assumed away all the possibilities that mean that one person can benefit at another's expense. If a person cannot improve his material position by theft or fraud or any other parasitic means, he can benefit himself only by engaging in trades that are mutually beneficial. He may not directly care about the well-being of others, but if he does not offer mutually beneficial trades, no one will trade with him. Competition ensures that one party to a trade cannot keep all the gains for himself. If one firm tries to raise prices well above costs, other firms will step in and drive prices down. The tendency for people to look for opportunities for mutually beneficial trade ensures the exploitation of all known opportunities for mutually beneficial trade, and the outcome will be socially optimal or efficient.

The term **efficiency**, extremely important in economics, refers to an allocation of goods that cannot be changed to make someone better off without making at least one other person worse off, when *better off* is defined as gaining something one wants and *worse off* is defined as losing something one wants. For example, assume a two-person economy that includes Dick and Jane. Dick has seven turnips, Jane has twelve, and turnips are the only good in this economy. Both would like to have more than they do now, but the only way for either of them to get another turnip would be for the other person to have one less. Thus the current allocation is efficient. Another name for efficiency is **Pareto efficiency.**[3] Given these conditions, market transactions lead to Pareto-efficient allocations.

Only much later, in the 1890s, was the theory of perfect competition developed and shown to illustrate a necessary condition for the market to achieve full efficiency. The proof can be shown graphically using the supply-and-demand graph. Compare figure 3.3 to figure 2.2. They look very much alike, and that is no coincidence. If the assumptions of perfect competition hold true, the demand curve represents the marginal benefit that consumers receive from using a good, and the supply curve represents the marginal cost that firms undergo in producing the good. Therefore, the equilibrium point is the point at which marginal benefit equals marginal cost, the optimal quantity not just for one individual but for all individuals in the market. If the quantity were less than the equilibrium quantity, marginal benefit would be less than marginal cost; consumers would be willing to pay more than the marginal cost of producing another unit, so it would be beneficial to society as a whole to produce another unit. If the quantity is greater than the equilibrium quantity, consumers are willing to pay less than the marginal cost of the last unit; thus the last unit was not worth what it cost to produce. Therefore, only the equilibrium quantity, the amount at which the marginal cost to produces equals the marginal benefit to consumers, is socially optimal.

For example, suppose Tom is a greedy capitalist. Tom cares about no one but himself, and his only ambition is to make himself as rich as possible. If Tom cannot defraud anyone, steal from anyone, cheat anyone, or extort anyone, then to benefit himself he has to find some way to entice others to trade with him. In other words, he has to offer them a trade that is mutually beneficial. He has no direct desire to make good products that other people want, but if he does not, no one will trade with him.

Because Tom has to offer mutually beneficial trades, he would at least like to jack the price up way above the marginal costs of producing and selling the goods so that he can capture most of the gains from these trades for himself. But if he does, a bunch of other greedy capitalists will see how much money he is making and enter the market. This increase in competition will force the price down to a level that reflects the marginal cost of producing and selling the good. None of the producers wants to sell the good for its marginal cost, but competition forces them to. When all the greedy capitalists in perfectly competitive markets are forced to sell their goods for the marginal costs, an allocation of goods results such that no redistribution of the goods in question can be completed without making at least one person worse off.

This was the invisible hand that led Smith to become a supporter of the doctrine of laissez-faire, which had originated in France some years earlier. Laissez-faire has been translated into English as "let it be," "to leave to do," or "hands off," and it means that the government should have no restrictions on trade, because a free market is one of the conditions necessary for the invisible hand to work. This may make you think that Smith must have been a radically conservative philosopher, but actually laissez faire was extremely liberal at the time. Today we think of government restrictions on trade as social policies aimed at helping the weak and the poor against big businesses. In Smith's day most government restrictions on trade were designed to give monopoly rights to politically powerful individuals. The idea that any commoner should be allowed to set up shop in any business he wanted was a new, liberal idea.

Laissez-faire quickly became a conservative doctrine after Smith's death, however, when business interests during the industrial revolution found they could use the theory of the invisible hand to oppose government efforts to create a better working environment or redistribute income. More than half a century after Smith's death, John Stuart Mill pointed out (in what is now known as the second fundamental theorem of welfare economics) that, although the invisible hand requires a given distribution of property rights, it does not depend on any *particular* distribution of property rights. Thus the government is free to change the distribution of property at the beginning and let the competitive market find the optimal quantity. Later authors have pointed out that redistributing property before transactions occur is difficult because the distribution of property at the beginning of any one day depends on the trades made the day before. Thus economists now debate the "efficiency-equity trade-off": If there are negative efficiency effects from redistributing property, what are they? How can they be minimized? And what amount of efficiency loss is a worthwhile price for more equity? The answers to these questions are highly controversial, but it is no longer sufficient to say simply that government should not redistribute property simply because it is inefficient.

Some have also tried to apply the theory of the invisible hand as an argument against government health, safety, and environmental regulations, but the argument does not always hold. No restrictions on trade is one of the necessary assumptions for the invisible hand to work, and thus for many years after Smith the invisible hand was rather simplistically applied to all government regulations. However, the theory of perfect competition has many assumptions, all of which must hold true for the outcome to be socially optimal and many of which often do not hold true. What has become known as the theory of second best is the recognition that if the first best outcome (a perfectly competitive market) does not exist, the next most efficient outcome may require the government to step in with a policy that eliminates or counteracts the failures of the market. Far from being a plank for a laissez-faire political platform, the perfectly competitive model can be used as a list of what is missing from real world markets.

Policy Application: Rent Control

Now we will apply some of the ideas that we have discussed in this chapter to a policy issue that is likely to be of great interest to social workers:

rent control. Rent control laws are on the books in a number of cities; New York City is the "rent control capital" of the nation. These laws regulate how much rent landlords can charge their tenants and are often advocated as a way to ensure that the poor and near poor will be able to afford housing. Given their professional concern for the impoverished, social workers are probably quite sympathetic to rent control laws. Economists, however, tend to oppose rent control laws because they argue that such laws tend to create shortages in rental housing markets and do not necessarily help the poor.

In figure 3.8 the equilibrium price is $250 and the equilibrium quantity is 6 million dwellings.[4] The authorities in Metropolis have passed a law that prevents landlords from raising rents higher than $150 a month. At this price the quantity demanded is 8 million dwellings, while quantity supplied is 4 million. Which is the quantity that will actually be rented when supply and demand are not equal? The guiding principle is known as short side rules: Firms may not be able to sell all they want, but they are not forced to sell any more than they want, and consumers may not be able to buy all they want, but they are not forced to buy any more than they want. Because the quantity that firms want to sell is the smaller of the two, landlords actually rent 4 million units, and Metropolis suffers a shortage of 4 million units. The rent control laws do make housing more affordable, but they do not make it more available. In fact, rent control laws make housing less available. Firms have less incentive to build new housing, and they even have an incentive to remove existing housing from the rental market. Those who live in the 4 million available rental units benefit from rent control, but rent control harms those who would be able to find a place if the price were allowed to rise to the equilibrium level.

Furthermore, rent control has a number of undesirable side effects. Firms may have less incentive to perform maintenance on buildings, and they find it easier to discriminate among renters. Consumers will be afraid to move if their needs change, and the difficulty of finding a vacant apartment will increase. We can also use supply and demand to find out what will happen to housing units that are not covered by rent control laws (such as those in nearby suburbs). Housing not subject to rent control is a substitute for rent-controlled housing; figure 3.4 reveals the answer. Demand will increase, and the equilibrium price and quantity will both increase. That is, efforts to control the rents on one type of housing will drive up prices for another type of housing, and thus rent control helps some consumers but hurts others.

FIGURE 3.8 Effect of a Rent Control Law

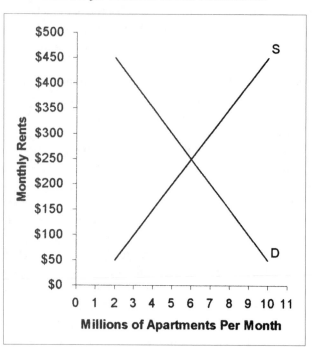

Because how a shortage of dwellings can help the poor, or anyone else for that matter, is not clear, economists tend not to think much of rent control laws as a way of ensuring access to housing. It is not enough to recognize a social problem; the solutions should be made as efficiently as possible. Rent control moves the outcome further from the efficient equilibrium so economists—even those who favor other means of making housing more affordable—generally frown upon it. If anything, economists are likely to argue that the poor be provided with housing subsidies. A housing subsidy would have the same effect as an increase in the supply of housing (see fig. 3.6), increasing the quantity sold and decreasing the price. Thus a subsidy would make housing not only more affordable but also more available. Another, more economical solution would be to redistribute income toward the poor so that they are able to afford housing at market prices.

Chapter Four

Imperfect Competition

As anyone who has ever dealt with a used car salesperson, tried to figure out which social worker or doctor to go to, or has lived in a company town knows, most markets are far from perfect. So what happens when the four assumptions of perfect competition—many buyers and sellers, an undifferentiated product, perfect information, and free entry and exit—are relaxed?

On the basis of differing assumptions, economists identify four other types of market structure: monopoly, monopsony, monopolistic competition, and oligopoly. None leads to all the desirable outcomes of perfect competition (the conditions of perfect competition do not obtain), so they are called **imperfectly competitive markets.** Each of these market structures has some unique characteristics, and knowledge of different structures is important for determining when, whether, and how government should intervene in the market.

Monopoly

The primary characteristic of a **monopoly** is that the market has only one seller. The following assumptions apply to the monopoly model:

1. *One seller and many buyers.* Only one firm sells this good in this market, which has many buyers, each too small to independently affect the monopolist's behavior.

2. *No close substitutes.* The monopolist's product is unique, and no products on the market are easily used in place of it.
3. *Perfect information.* The seller and all buyers know the prices and quantities of goods in the market.
4. *Barriers to entry.* New firms find that entering the market is either difficult or impossible.

As we'll see, if these assumptions hold, the firm has the power to set price, the firm can make economic profits even in the long run, and the industry is inefficient. We will also explore policy responses to monopoly.

In a monopoly one firm sells a product for which no close substitutes exist. Examples of monopolies include the local telephone and local cable television providers in most areas of the United States. Small markets might have monopolies in industries that usually are not considered monopolies. A small town might have only one grocery store, one gas station, or one social worker in private practice. Although their products are not unusual, these firms are considered monopolies because their product is unique in their market. Every firm in some sense competes with other firms; if you are feeling stressed you can see a massage therapist instead of a social worker. Therefore, the situation is not one of no substitutes for a monopoly's product, just that there are no *close* substitutes. Thus the line dividing monopolies from other types of markets is a bit fuzzy. The cable television company is the only provider of certain channels, but it competes with satellite and broadcast television. Is it a monopolist? It probably is because most consumers do not consider these alternatives to be close substitutes for cable television. McDonald's is the only company that sells a Big Mac, but it competes with Burger King, Roy Rogers, and many other restaurants. Is it a monopolist? It probably isn't because these other restaurants, although they do not produce Big Macs, produce goods that are easily substituted for McDonald's products. Is a massage therapist really a substitute for the only social worker in a small town? The answer may depend on what is ailing the client. A massage therapist may be a close substitute if the problem is stress but may not be if low self-esteem is the culprit.

In order for a monopolized market to stay that way permanently, it must have some barriers to entry that keep other sellers out. These barriers can be created by the firm, legally and otherwise, or they may be cost advantages. A company creates barriers when it tries to establish itself as a monopoly by making it difficult for other firms to compete. This practice is illegal in the United States. Legal barriers are government laws that allow only one firm to compete in a market. Such barriers exist for some cable television companies, power companies, and other industries. It might seem strange that the government would create barriers for some firms while it prosecutes other firms that erect their own barriers, but it often creates legal barriers for industries that are believed to be natural monopolies. A **natural monopoly** exists when a single large firm can produce at lower cost than smaller firms can. The natural monopoly is an industry for which the law of diminishing returns does not hold—or, more precisely, the law of diminishing returns does not set in at the quantity demanded. Thus larger firms will always outcompete smaller firms until only one firm is left in the market. In such an industry a competitive equilibrium cannot exist, and only one firm can exist in the long run. Suppose, for example, that Small Town, U.S.A., has two bus companies, the Main Street Line and the Elm Street Line. Main Street is bigger than Elm Street, that is, it provides service to more riders. Main Street's cost per rider is $1.00 and it charges each rider $2.25. Thus its profit per rider is $1.25. Elm Street's cost per rider is $2.20 and it too charges each rider $2.25, leaving it a profit per rider of $0.05. Clearly, Main Street can drive Elm Street out of the market by charging any price greater than $1.00 and less than $2.20 because it could still make a profit, whereas Elm Street could not.

Price-setting, or market, power is the ability of a single buyer or firm to influence price through its purchase or sale of a good. Consumers in a competitive market have the choice of buying from one firm or any other firm, so any one firm has a limited ability to charge more than its competitors. But because a monopolist has no close competitors, consumers' choice is limited to buying from the one firm or not buying at all. This gives the firm a great deal of leeway to set its price. You many think that a monopolist will therefore sell its goods at the highest price that consumers will pay, but this conclusion is too simple; it forgets that every consumer is different. No one maximum price exists at which consumers buy a given amount and above which consumers buy none at all. When the price goes up, some consumers will not change their behavior at all, some will buy a little less, and others may stop buying altogether. Thus the demand curve has its familiar downward-sloping shape. The monopolist can raise the price, but if it does so, it must accept that consumers, on average, will buy a little less. So if it raises the price, it will gain in revenue per unit, but it will lose in the number of units sold. If the monopolist lowers the price to nearly zero, it will have a very high quantity, but the price will be so low that the company will not make any money. Some price is so high that hardly anyone will buy, and the firm will again make almost no money even though its price will be very high. The firm's goal is to find that price that maximizes profit.

The monopolist can sustain **long-run economic profits** because of its price-setting ability and because new firms find that entering the market is difficult or impossible. The firm's price-setting ability allows it to choose any price to maximize profit, and often this means making a profit (although it does not necessarily ensure profits). Normally, economic profits attract entry from other firms until those profits are competed away, but in a monopoly barriers to entry prevent this process from happening. Thus, if a monopolist is profitable, it can stay profitable indefinitely. Social workers might regard sustained profits as unfair, especially if a monopolist makes positive economic profits from a good that people need. Suppose a monopolist sells food, housing, health care, or electricity. This would mean that people would have to pay more for these items not because they cost more to produce but simply because sellers could get away with charging them more.

The inefficiency of a monopoly follows from the firm's price-setting ability. This allows it to increase the price above the perfectly competitive price, but consumers respond by buying less than the perfectly competitive quantity. (The technical aspects of how a monopolist sets its price are irrelevant to this discussion.) It is sufficient to say that, because the monopolist has price-setting power, its price is always higher and the quantity traded always lower than either would be in a perfectly competitive market. Figure 4.1 illustrates the inefficiency of the monopoly.

Because the competitive equilibrium quantity is efficient, any other quantity is inefficient. The loss in quantity, not the high price, makes monopoly inefficient. High prices may make it unfair but not inefficient. Remember that efficiency is about the total amount of goods available to society, not about who gets those goods. A monopolist does not really want to limit the quantity; it accepts a lower quantity only so that it can charge a higher price. Both consumers and the firm lose out because the

FIGURE 4.1 **The Inefficient Monopolist**

The monopolist's price (P_M) is higher and its output (Q_M) is lower than the perfectly competitive equilibrium price and quantity (P_{PC} and Q_{PC}). Because the perfectly competitive output is socially optimal, the monopolist's output must be suboptimal. The perfectly competitive output equates marginal benefit with marginal cost, but the monopolist's profit-maximizing quantity does not.

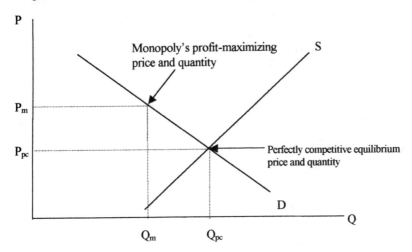

quantity is reduced. The firm makes up for this loss and more because it receives a higher price, but consumers lose out a second time because of the higher price. Thus we know that the gain that the firm receives from charging a higher price is smaller than the consumers' loss and therefore the monopoly outcome is inefficient.

Another way to understand the inefficiency is to remember that at the competitive equilibrium, price equals marginal cost, so the price paid by consumers equals the cost to society of producing the good. Because a monopoly has a lower quantity, it receives a higher price and has a lower cost. For example, a monopolist in the textbook industry sells books for $85 each, although the marginal cost is only $25. The marginal benefit of the book is $85, but society would only have to forgo $25 worth of other goods to produce each book. Therefore, the laws of rational decision making imply that more books would be beneficial to society, but the monopolist will not produce more because that would force it to lower its price and reduce its profit.

Another inefficiency caused by monopolies is that they can get away with imposing higher nonpecuniary costs on buyers.[1] For example, suppose a small local market for counseling had just one provider of psychotherapy. Clients who went to this provider's office might have to spend long periods in waiting areas. This would be time that the clients could have spent engaging in other useful activities, so their waiting time would be a cost. The therapist might be able to do some things to decrease clients' waits, but as a monopolist, the therapist faces no competitive pressure to do any of them.

A government has three things it can do to alleviate the inefficiency caused by monopolies. First, it can attempt to foster competition in monopolistic markets by breaking up monopolies or by preventing them from forming. This is why the United States has antitrust laws. Antitrust laws limit mergers (the joining together of firms to create bigger firms) between firms that sell goods in the same market. Antitrust laws also limit price-fixing between firms in the same market; that is, they prevent competing firms from acting as if they were a monopolist (see the discussion of cartels later in this chapter). The U.S. government used antitrust laws to break up American Telephone and Telegraph's monopoly on long-distance phone service, and the Justice Department has taken Microsoft to court.

Second, governments may choose to allow the monopoly to exist but regulate its price. The U.S. government has used this solution for phone companies and electricity companies, and local governments sometimes use it for cable television. This option is usually used for industries that are believed to be natural monopolies. Breaking up a natural monopoly would not work very well because a group of smaller firms would have a higher cost than one large firm would. But leaving the natural monopolist alone usually is not a good idea because natural monopolies have the same desire to maximize profit as any other firm, so they will raise prices above costs and may raise prices well above costs. For example, you may think your water bill is high now, but how high would your bill have to go before you seriously considered drilling a well? You would probably let it go quite high. Thus, if the water company were an unregulated monopolist, it could get away with a very high price. It is difficult for government to determine the "right" price to allow a natural monopolist to charge, and firms that face a regulated price have efficiency problems, but regulation may be the best solution, given the alternatives.

Third, the government could simply take the monopoly over and run it itself. The U.S. government has used this solution in a number of industries, including passenger rail service, the highway system, and the postal service. This strategy is more common in Europe. The disadvantage of this approach is that it is difficult for the government to determine the most efficient price and the most efficient forms of management. But the advantage is that any profit that the monopoly makes could be used for other government projects that are beneficial to society as a whole.

Monopsony

Monopsony, in a way, is the reverse of monopoly. A monopoly has many buyers and one seller, while a **monopsony** has many sellers and one buyer. Thus it is the buyer who has the power to set price. The monopsonist (the buyer in a monopsony) uses its market power to set a low price rather than a higher price. Otherwise, the results are similar to the results of the monopoly model. The following assumptions apply to the monopsony model:

1. *One buyer and many sellers.* One buyer snaps up all the goods sold in this market from many small sellers who cannot independently affect the monopsonist's behavior.
2. *Homogeneous product.* Sellers in this market sell an identical product.
3. *Perfect information.* The sellers and buyer know the prices and quantities of goods in the market.
4. *Barriers to entry.* Buyers face barriers to entry, and sellers face barriers to exit.

Again, we will spare you the technical aspects of how a monopsonist chooses the profit-maximizing price and just say that both price and quantity are lower than they would be in a perfectly competitive market. Figure 4.2 shows the inefficiency of the industry.

The most commonly cited example of a monopsony is a small town with one large employer. Because the town has only one buyer of labor, those who want to work have to sell their labor to this buyer or leave town. Note that the monopsonist hires less labor than a competitive firm would.

FIGURE 4.2 The Inefficient Monopsonist

The monopsonist's price (P_M) and quantity (Q_M) are both lower than the perfectly competitive equilibrium price and quantity (P_{PC} and Q_{PC}). Because the perfectly competitive quantity is socially optimal, the monopsonist's quantity is not.

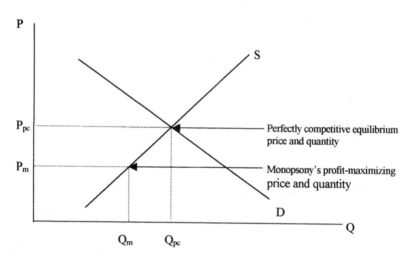

The firm does not really want to buy less labor. It accepts a lower quantity in order to obtain a lower price, because fewer workers are willing to accept the very low wages that a monoponsist pays. In fact, the firm would be willing to buy much more labor at this price (read across to the demand curve) if workers were willing to accept it. Or the firm would be willing to pay much more for this quantity of labor (read up to the demand curve), but it would do so only if competitive pressure forced it to. The monopsonist uses its market power to set the wage below workers' marginal product. In other words, workers are paid less than they are worth. This is arguably exploitation, and those, like social workers, who believe that government ought to promote justice, would probably argue that government policy should be to curtail exploitation to the extent that it exists. Those who are interested in promoting efficiency would also be interested in curtailing the power of monopsonists. A monopsonist is not inefficient because of the low wages but because of the lower quantity.

So what strategies work to curtail the monopsonist? Suppose a small town had just one social service agency. Social workers in this town would be able to get a job with only this employer. The monopsony model predicts that the employer would higher fewer social workers than a competitive agency and would pay the workers less than their marginal product (perhaps measured by the number of clients that a social worker counsels per hour).

The theory of second best applies in any situation in which the market fails to achieve an efficient level of output. Two strategies that can hurt efficiency in a perfectly competitive market can increase efficiency in a monopsony—the minimum wage and unionization. Either of these can function as a substitute for competitive pressure to force the firm to pay a higher wage and may thus bring the market closer to the efficient quantity.

Monopolistic Competition

Like perfectly competitive markets, monopolistically competitive markets have many small buyers and sellers, free entry and exit, and perfect information (although perfect information is not as essential to monopolistic competition as it is to perfect competition). The difference between the two market structures is that perfectly competitive markets have a homogeneous product and monopolistically competitive markets have a differentiated product. That is, every firm in a perfectly competitive industry produces a product that is identical to the product of every other firm, but every firm in a monopolistically competitive industry produces a product that has some unique characteristics but is a close substitute for the products of other firms. Examples of monopolistic competition are typically found in retail industries. For example, one restaurant's food is not exactly like another's, but the restaurants are close substitutes for each other. One brewery's beer is not exactly like another's, but they are close substitutes. One social worker in private practice is not exactly like another, but they are close substitutes. One social worker may provide Jungian therapy, while another may provide Freudian. One social worker might have a slightly different style than another, although all arguably provide the same basic type of service.

Product differentiation gives each firm some power to set its own price. But monopolistically competitive firms typically have less price-setting power than monopolies because close substitutes are available. This is because the demand curve facing a monopolistically competitive firm is more elastic than the demand curve facing a monopolist. That is, the quantity demanded is more responsive to price changes in monopolistically competitive markets than in monopolies. Free entry and exit prevent monopolistically competitive firms from getting much benefit out of their price-setting power. If they make economic profit, competitors will enter the industry, lowering the demand for each individual firm's product until profits equal zero. Thus a monopolistically competitive firm sells a smaller quantity at a higher price than would a perfectly competitive firm. Is a monopolistically competitive industry less efficient than a competitive industry? Not necessarily, because monopolistic competition offers something that benefits consumers—more choices—that at least partially counteracts the negative effects of higher prices. Would you like to live in a world where all restaurants, all beer, and all social workers were exactly the same? This is what would be necessary to create perfect competition in these industries. If perfect competition were created, you might be able to get these products a little cheaper than you can now, but would you be willing to give up the variety in order to spend less money? The answer may depend on how much cheaper and how good the homogeneous products were. No one knows for sure whether the benefit of more variety is greater or smaller than the loss resulting from inefficient production, and therefore no one can say whether a monopolistically competitive industry is less efficient than perfect competition.

Oligopoly

Oligopolistic markets are in between competitive markets and monopolies. This market has a small number of firms. The word *small* is used here in a technical sense. It does not mean a specific number of firms but that the number of firms is *small enough* so that each firm has some power to influence the market price and noticeably affect its competitors. The following assumptions sum up the **oligopoly** model:

1. *Small number of sellers and many buyers.* This market has so few sellers that the decisions of each noticeably affect the sales of others, and at least some sellers can influence market price.
2. *Homogeneous or different products.* The product offered for sale may be homogeneous or differentiated.

3. *Imperfect information.* There is perfect information regarding prices, but firms do not have perfect information regarding rivals' reactions.
4. *Barriers to entry.* Barriers hinder new firms from entering the market.

A few large firms dominate oligopolistic markets, although the market may have some small competitors as well. The product may be homogeneous or differentiated. For example, a few large firms dominate the steel industry. All steel is not the same, but even if all steel were identical, the steel industry would be no less an oligopoly. Two large firms (Pepsi and Coke) each produce many products that are not exactly alike, and they dominate the soda industry. Consumers are assumed to have perfect information about the products and prices available, and firms are assumed to have perfect information about past prices charged by other firms, but they do not know how other firms will react if they change their own strategy. Barriers to entry exist so that the few firms in the industry are fairly sure that new firms cannot enter the industry and compete at the same scale.

The outcome of an oligopoly is uncertain. Firms are large enough to influence the market price, but whether they do depends on how much competition is provided by the other firms in the industry. In competitive markets new firms entering the market mean that all firms cannot sustain economic profits. Entry is insufficient to ensure long-run zero profits in an oligopoly, but competition among existing firms may or may not be enough to keep profits near zero. The quantity therefore may or may not be lower than the perfectly competitive quantity, and thus the industry may or may not be inefficient.

These outcomes are uncertain because oligopoly behavior is strategic. A competitive firm simply reacts to a predictable market price. A monopolist reacts to a predictable market demand curve, but oligopolistic firms have to react to the unpredictable action of other firms. They must choose their strategy based on an estimate of the other firms' strategies, but other firms will change their strategy in reaction to changes in the first firm's strategy. Thus the operation of an oligopoly is more like a game and more uncertain than any other market structure.

What can be said about the consequences of oligopolies? At one extreme the price could be as high and the quantity as low as in a monopoly; at the other extreme the price could be as low and the quantity as high as in a perfectly competitive industry. Of course, the consequences could be anywhere between these extremes. Oligopolies have more incentive than other firms to compete on the basis of factors other than product and price, such as advertising—a situation known as **nonprice competition**—but economists have not been able to ascertain whether advertising increases or decreases efficiency. More than that cannot be said with certainty, but there are several ways that oligopolies might behave, and economists have several different methods to model their behavior. Firms in an oligopoly may compete as if they were perfectly competitive firms and reach the competitive outcome. This outcome, however, is probably unlikely because it relies on firms' ignoring the market power that they have. Firms could take their competitors' strategy as given and set their own strategy based on the assumption that other firms will not change their strategy. If all firms do this, the industry will reach an equilibrium of sorts in which no firm has an incentive to change its behavior so long as no other firm changes its behavior, but this equilibrium will not be the perfectly competitive equilibrium.

Oligopolists could band together into a cartel and behave as if they were one big monopolist. If firms in an oligopoly choose this strategy, they make arrangements to set prices, output levels, sales territories, and so forth. If successful, the industry would have the same inefficiency associated with monopolies, but cartels might not be successful for long for several reasons. Most important, in the United States forming a cartel is illegal. The executives of firms that do so are subject to imprisonment or a fine under the U.S. antitrust laws.[2]

Legalities aside, individual cartel members have an incentive to break the agreement. As a group, firms have an incentive to make a cartel agreement that restricts output to achieve a higher price so that each can make a share of the monopoly profits. But any one firm can make even more money if it breaks the agreement, cuts its price a little, and captures a larger share of monopoly profits. Because all firms have this incentive, the agreement may break down entirely. For example, suppose Jill, Betty, and Wilma were the only psychotherapists in Mudville. Jill, Betty, and Wilma have agreed that if each provides only twenty sessions a week instead of the usual forty, they can charge $200 a session instead of their usual $50. Thus they can each increase their income from $2,000 a week to $4,000 while working half as much. One day it occurs to Betty that if she lowers her price while Jill and Wilma stick to the cartel price, some of their clients will come to her, allowing her to make an even higher profit. She sees forty patients a week for $150 each, making $6,000. But this cuts into Jill's and Wilma's profits, so they cut their price to get those clients back, and pretty soon all three are back to charging $50 a session and seeing forty clients.

Cartels are also unstable because they attract entry into the market. Entry is difficult in an oligopoly but not necessarily impossible. It is in the interest of cartel members to keep new entrants out of the market or to get them to join the cartel agreement if they get in. But these actions are illegal and difficult to maintain. One way to discourage entry is to advertise so that new firms will have to undertake a great expense to make a dent in the market. Another is not to charge the full monopoly price so that the economic profits are not as high as they could be and do not attract as much entry. But this strategy brings the industry closer to the competitive level.

Oligopolists may coordinate their behavior like a cartel without an explicit agreement. One way to do this is though **price leadership**—one firm sets a price and other firms in the industry follow. This is simply implicit price-fixing and may simply be a way that firms can make cartel profits without being subject to prosecution. Sometimes this implicit form of price-fixing is accompanied by nonprice competition. That is, firms pursuing similar pricing practices compete with one another on the basis of packaging differences, quality differences, or differences regarding offers of special services. This type of situation occurs frequently in the real world, and economists have given a lot of attention to it.

Because oligopoly behavior is uncertain and the available strategies are many, economists have used game theory to analyze oligopolies.[3] **Game theory** is a branch of mathematics used by social scientists to study strategic interactions between or among firms, people, and other parties; it models a strategic situation as a game and is sometimes studied by having research subjects play the game for money. Game theory thus far, however, still leads to the conclusion that the outcome in an oligopoly is uncertain.

The most common policy response to oligopoly in the United States is for regulators to try to prevent the formation of cartels. Regulators have the power to review mergers to prevent firms from becoming so large that they can dominate a market, but they have generally used this power only to prevent markets from becoming monopolies, not to prevent markets from becoming oligopolized or to prevent oligopolies from becoming more concentrated. Recent mergers have cut the number of large firms dominating some industries in half with little interference from regulators.

An Application: Health Care

One of the most controversial trends in the health-care industry is the increasing number of health-insurance carriers whose policies mandate managed care. The health-care premiums of many of these people are subsidized by their employers, whereas others must pay their premiums entirely from their own pockets. Suppose the health-insurance market were an oligopoly made up of four managed care firms. If these firms were to form a cartel, implicitly fix prices, or engage in other types of coordination, the market could develop features of a monopoly.

A monopoly-like health-insurance market would lead to inefficient consequences. Employers and individuals would end up paying premiums that exceed the marginal cost of providing coverage. The result would be a suboptimal amount of health-insurance coverage and positive economic profits for members of the cartel. Health insurance is, arguably, something people need. Thus health-insurance companies would be making positive economic profits at the expense of the many who would either have to go without a necessity or pay much more for it than would be necessary in another market situation. The inefficiency and injustice associated with a monopolistic health-insurance market could serve as the basis for government intervention. This intervention could take the form of antitrust actions, government regulation of managed care companies' premiums, subsidies to help consumers purchase health insurance, or nationalization. Chapter 10 includes a more thorough discussion of health care.

This chapter has focused on market structures because the inefficiency and injustice associated with some types of market structures are the most important justifications for government intervention. Table 4.1 provides a concise summary of the market structures and their characteristics. The next chapter focuses on other problems that can arise from sole reliance on market allocation of goods.

TABLE 4.1 **A Summary of the Five Types of Market Structures**

	Perfect competition	Monopoly	Monopsony	Monopolistic Competition	Oligopoly
ASSUMPTIONS	1. Many buyers and sellers. 2. Undifferentiated product. 3. Perfect information. 4. Free entry and exit.	1. One seller, many buyers. 2. Unique product with no close substitutes. 3. Perfect information. 4. Barriers to entry.	1. Many sellers, one buyer. 2. Differentiated or undifferentiated product. 3. Perfect information. 4. Barriers to entry for buyers, barriers to exit for sellers.	1. Many buyers and sellers. 2. Differentiated product. 3. Perfect or imperfect information. 4. Free entry and exit.	1. Few sellers, many buyers. 2. Differentiated or undifferentiated product. 3. Imperfect information. 4. Barriers to entry.
RESULTS	1. Law of one price holds. Firms are price takers. 2. No economic profits in the long run. 3. Efficient.	1. Seller has price-setting power. 2. Economic profits can exist. 3. Inefficient.	1. Buyer has price-setting power. 2. Economic profits can exist indefinitely. 3. Inefficient.	1. Firms have some price-setting power. 2. No economic profits. 3. Uncertain efficiency.	1. Uncertain pricing. 2. Uncertain profits. 3. Uncertain efficiency.

Chapter Five

Market Failure and Government Intervention

Conservatives certainly disagree, but theoretical justification exists for government intervention in markets. Still, readers of all political stripes may well wonder: Isn't a government decision justified so long as it is made democratically? At least two arguments—one based on the principle of liberty and the other on the principle of efficiency—commonly are offered for why the government should not intervene in the economy unless it has a compelling reason to do so.

The liberty argument against government intervention is that people have a right to exchange their legally owned property for whatever they see fit. A government restriction on people's ability to make free use of their property—even a restriction approved by majority vote—represents an imposition on individual freedom and as such should be avoided unless the reason to do otherwise is compelling. Because this is not a book on ethics or political philosophy, we'll end the discussion of the liberty argument here.

The efficiency argument against government intervention is based on economists' understanding of the benefits associated with perfectly competitive markets. Recall from chapter 3 that, barring distortions, perfectly competitive markets result in efficient allocations of goods. As discussed in chapter 3, the idea that the entire society benefits from exchanges between selfish individuals in perfectly competitive markets is now called the first fundamental theorem of welfare economics (FFTWE).[1]

The FFTWE does not seem to leave a lot of room for government to make a positive contribution, but one important avenue for government intervention is available. Recall from chapter 1 that one function of government in mixed economies is affecting the distribution of property rights. If society regards a particular distribution of property as too unequal, it can use taxes and transfers to alter this distribution.[2] After doing so, if the government allows people to engage in trades with one another and markets are perfectly competitive, the resulting allocation of goods will be Pareto efficient. This conclusion is the second fundamental theorem of welfare economics, and it shows that government intervention aimed at creating a more equal distribution of property need not necessarily interfere with economic efficiency.[3]

Occasionally, you will hear people use the FFTWE as part of an oversimplified argument against government intervention in the economy. It goes like this: Because one condition for an efficient outcome is the existence of markets with free entry and exit, and because government intervention can restrict entry, markets without government intervention are more efficient than ones with government intervention. This argument is fallacious because it ignores the fact that many other conditions for an efficient outcome also are not met. It amounts to saying that even though all the conditions needed for efficiency are not met, we should meet as many of them as possible. But according to a perspective in economics called the theory of the second best (TSB), meeting many but not all conditions for efficiency does not lead to efficient markets. The TSB states that if some conditions for efficiency are not met, violating another condition for efficiency may be necessary in order to counteract the first. Because all the conditions for an efficient economy rarely are met, the theory of the second best implies that government has many opportunities to intervene to promote the efficiency of the economy. For example, if the assumption of perfect information (see chapter 3) is not met, the government could promote efficiency by providing information to consumers.

Market failure occurs when one condition necessary for Pareto efficiency is absent. If the market fails, the market outcome is inefficient; the government could enact policies that lead to a **Pareto improvement**, a change in the allocation of goods that makes at least one person better off without making anyone worse off. In this chapter we discuss potential market failures and what government might do to address them. Imperfect competition, discussed in chapter 4, is a kind of market failure.

Externalities

Probably the most common example of market failure is an **externality** (also known as **external effects**, or **third-party effects**), which is an effect of market exchanges on people who are not a party to those exchanges. Every transaction has costs and benefits. So long as only the buyers and sellers feel these costs and benefits, they can determine the optimal amount to trade. But if trades between buyers and sellers affect someone else, costs or benefits will exist that the buyers and sellers are unaware of or are uninterested in, and these effects will not be figured into the decision of how much to buy or produce. Therefore, the amounts chosen by buyers and sellers, though they may be optimal from their private perspectives, are not optimal from a social perspective.[4]

A classic example of an externality is pollution. If Michael buys a car from Roger, he evaluates the benefit of his enjoyment of the car against the price he has to pay for the car. Roger evaluates the price he receives for the car against the cost of producing the car. But other costs exist that neither of them has considered. The engine will produce gas fumes, and rubber will rub off the tires and enter the environment. The amount of pollution caused by Michael's car is negligible to him and to Roger, but it is not negligible to society in general. Such pollution is undoubtedly responsible for many respiratory and other health problems that medical social workers often see. If the external costs of pollution are not internalized (considered), buyers and sellers of automobiles will not choose the socially optimal level of automobile production. Costs are internalized when society has found a way to make market participants feel external costs.

The externality concept is related to another current policy debate. Many motorists talk on cell phones while driving. Some people believe that such motorists are as dangerous as drunk drivers and contend that government should regulate cell phone use by motorists. According to Robert W. Hahn, an analyst affiliated with the American Enterprise Institute, a conservative think tank, some states are beginning to regulate this behavior. Hahn thinks such regulation is not justified, in part because he believes that drivers should decide whether they want to accept the small chance of dying in a car accident while talking on a cell phone in order to attain whatever gains they receive from their conversations.[5]

The problem with Hahn's position is that it assumes that all those who die as a result of someone's driving while talking on a cell phone are those who made the choice to talk while driving. But what if, as is likely to be the case, some of those who die are not talking on the cell phone? What if they are struck by someone talking on a cell phone? Or are a passenger in the phone user's car? Those who use cell phones while driving may consider only the potential costs and benefits of this behavior to themselves, not to other parties who die in accidents that the phone users have caused. In other words, motorists using cell phones probably impose external costs; therefore, government regulation of some kind could be justified.

The renowned sociologist James S. Coleman applied economic tools to the study of sociological issues.[6] In his widely acclaimed book *Foundations of Social Theory,* he uses the term *externality* a bit more broadly than economists typically do. Economists tend to focus on how consumption, production, and market transactions affect third parties.[7] Coleman's conception includes external effects of behaviors not ordinarily considered to be consumption, production, or market exchanges.[8] For example, suppose José is a social worker who disapproves of child abuse. In the supermarket one day he sees a mother brutally slap her child. The woman has chosen to do this after weighing the benefits and costs to her (presumably, one benefit is that it gets her child to behave). Yet her action, within Coleman's broader conception of externality, negatively affects José's utility. The slapping of the child, in a sense, "pollutes" José's environment.

There are probably many, like José, who do not like child abuse, and many who abuse children without considering the external costs of this behavior. Government systems of child welfare can be justified as mechanisms for addressing the negative externalities caused by child abuse and neglect. That a father might lose custody of his children as a consequence of abusing them might encourage him to consider the external cost of child maltreatment.

The problem with Coleman's analysis is that it makes it very difficult to draw the line between externalities and nonexternalities. Suppose José is offended by public displays of affection. If he walks into a shopping mall and sees a man and woman kissing each other, he will feel his environment has been polluted. Would the government be justified if it passed a law prohibiting public displays of affection? Many, including many social workers, would say no. Most economists would also probably say no, because they believe that discussion of externalities should be limited to those who are directly affected in their persons or property. Society bans child abuse because of concern for the child, not for José.

The externalities we have described thus far are negative externalities because the behaviors impose cost on third parties. In the case of a positive externality, an action generates a benefit to a third party. One example would be a new building that makes the city a more beautiful place. Social workers could help clients recover from mental illnesses and thereby benefit not only themselves and their clients but also society in general. Because people with mental illnesses are sometimes violent, other members of society benefit from a decrease in the probability that they will become victims of violent crimes committed by people with such illnesses.

Not all negative effects are externalities. Secondhand smoke is an externality, but if cigarette smoke is dangerous only to the person who smokes, this is not an externality. It may be an informational problem, if the smoker is not aware of how dangerous smoking really is. It may be a psychological problem, if the smoker does not care about her own health. But any of the health consequences of smoking that affect only the smoker are not externalities. The costs of the health effects of smoke can be an externality, however, if the smoker herself does not pay for them. Cigarette smokers, with the help of manufacturers, damage their health, leaving governments to pay for the necessary treatment in the form of Medicare and Medicaid. Hence, though the dangers of cigarettes are not inherently an externality, they have become one because we do not ask every individual to pay the full cost of his own health care.

When externalities arise, the outcomes of market transactions are inefficient. Thus government would be justified if it intervened in the market to increase efficiency. In the case of negative externalities, such as pollution, this usually takes the form of banning the release of certain chemicals into the environment, limiting the emissions allowed by each firm, or mandating the use of specific kinds of pollution-control devices. Economists, however, usually suggest a more market-oriented approach that would internalize the cost of the externality. The government could tax firms for every unit of pollution created that reflects the cost of pollution to society. Thus the more a firm pollutes, the more it would pay in taxes. The advantage of this approach is that it allows the firm flexibility in how it reacts to the problem. That is, a firm could choose the method that would be most cost-effective in reducing pollution. This approach, of course, raises the difficult question of how to determine the costs to society of an externality, but the government could always err on the side of caution and set the externality tax on the high side.

Governments have a number of different ways to deal with positive externalities as well. These include subsidies, direct government provision, and regulation. Suppose Ricky is a twenty-nine-year-old homeless man with tuberculosis. Given that tuberculosis is highly contagious, if Ricky purchased treatment, a positive externality would result. In an effort to promote this positive externality, the government could do a number of things. It could build public clinics that provide free tuberculosis treatment. It could subsidize Ricky's treatment by giving him the money to pay for it. Or government could enact a law that requires all physicians to provide treatment, free of charge, to indigent people with tuberculosis.

Public Goods

Another example of market failure is a public good. A **public good** is a good that is available to everyone. This is actually a rather extreme form of a positive externality.[9] A classic example has to do with a group of mice who decide that the best way to avoid being harmed by a cat is to hang a bell around its neck so they can hear its approach. The problem is that they cannot decide who will actually hang the bell. If any one mouse were to successfully place the bell around the cat's neck, all the other mice would benefit just as much as the one who did the work. Thus each mouse has an incentive not to do the work. Why would a particular mouse agree to risk life and limb by trying to place a bell around the cat's neck when he could just wait for some other mouse to do the job and still benefit? The problem is that if all the mice think this way, none of them will be willing to hang the bell. Thus something that they all value (being protected from the cat) would simply not happen.

Perhaps the mice could solve this problem if they pooled their resources and paid a mouse to hang the bell. As long as enough mice contributed to this project to get it done, all mice would benefit, whether they contributed or not. But why would any one mouse contribute? Once again, each mouse would ask herself, "Why should I contribute when I could just wait for the others to do so and still benefit?" And once again, if all mice think this way, the cat can still sneak up on them. The deal in which all the other mice pay one mouse a fee to hang the bell around the cat's neck is a kind of market transaction. Because of this kind of problem, the market either may not produce public goods or may not be produce them at their optimal level. This is called the free-rider problem, and it extends beyond imaginary societies made up of mice and aggressive felines. Markets rarely ensure efficient levels of the production of public goods.

For example, Michael Tanner is a contemporary social analyst who has argued that the federal government should get out of the business of providing income support to the poor.[10] Tanner believes that if his proposal were enacted, the poor would not suffer because private individuals would contribute enough through private charities to meet the needs of the poor. The private charity solution is a market approach to aiding the poor. People would donate money to some charity, and in return the charity would see to it that the poor have the money or goods they need. It should not be too difficult to see that the free-rider problem would arise here as well.

Assume that a large portion of the population, if not everyone, wants to live in a nation with less poverty. The evidence for this is that many do contribute to charities. But most people probably benefit from living in a society without poverty, not from personally contributing to charity to reduce poverty. Thus under a system of private charity many people might decide to wait for someone else to donate because they could benefit anyway. As a result, many would not contribute, and many of the poor would remain needy. The free-rider problem in charity can be addressed by making a binding agreement that all people will donate some portion of their income to the poor. The only way to make this agreement binding on all members of the populace, however, would be to make it a law. Thus the redistribution of income through a democratic electoral process can be viewed as people making an agreement that says, "I'll do my part to help the poor if you do yours."

U.S. society treats many goods as public goods, although technically they are not. Free public education is available to all children in the United States. No one is excluded for nonpayment of taxes, although it would be possible for public schools to charge tuition and exclude all those who did not pay their share. We also treat libraries and freeways as public goods, although we could treat them otherwise. We could set up tolls all along freeways and charge membership fees for all libraries.

Imperfect Information

The model of perfect competition assumes that buyers and sellers have perfect knowledge of the quality of goods exchanged, of the prices available for similar goods for sale elsewhere, and of all information that might be relevant to their decisions to buy or sell goods. If this assumption does not hold, market outcomes are not as likely to be efficient. Information problems often involve **asymmetric information,** which means that one party to a transaction has relevant information that the other party does not and so has the opportunity to manipulate the transaction. This type of problem can prevent mutually beneficial exchanges from taking place. One of the most frequent results of asymmetric information is **adverse selection,** which occurs when asymmetric information about the quality of what is being exchanged causes the exchange of a suboptimal amount.[11] Another frequent result of asymmetric information is **moral hazard,** which occurs when being insured against some risk provides an incentive to engage in behaviors that increase the likelihood that the risky event will occur.[12]

Have you ever wondered why private companies will insure people against so many kinds of risks—death, sickness, fire, flood, theft, and many others—but no private insurance company will insure against unemployment or a sudden unexpected decrease in a person's income? Certainly, people would like to insure themselves against this kind of risk just as they insure themselves against other types. A market for income insurance does not exist for two important reasons.

First, people who know they are insured have an incentive to engage in more risky behavior. For example, workers who know they are insured against income loss may shirk more on the job, miss work more frequently, spend money more frivolously, and so on. All these behaviors would increase the likelihood of the event insured against (loss of income), which would be costly to insurance companies (moral hazard). If insurance against an event causes individuals to behave in ways that make the event more likely to occur, the cost of providing insurance will become greater and may make insurance prohibitively expensive.

Second, individuals have much better information about the likelihood of losing their jobs than insurance companies do. Thus, if these companies were to base the premium for income insurance on the probability that the average person would lose her income, only those with an above-average risk would buy the insurance. Insurance companies would then find that their revenues were on average not covering the amounts that they had to pay in claims. This would lead them to raise their premiums. But then only those who have the highest risk of losing their income would still find income insurance worth buying at the new, higher price. People who have relatively lower risk would drop their insurance, which would in turn decrease revenues of insurance companies. This would again cause insurance companies to increase their premiums. This cycle would continue until the premiums were so high that no one would buy insurance (adverse selection). This is a complete market failure because there is a risk that people would like to insure against, but no private market could develop to insure against this type of risk. One solution might be to take away the option to drop the policy—either by mandating the purchase of insurance or by the government's providing income insurance. This is part of the justification for government unemployment insurance, food stamps, Temporary Assistance to Needy Families, and other government income-maintenance programs.

Insurance companies engage in a behavior that may appear to be moral hazard but is not. Health-insurance companies are often accused of selling insurance only to those who do not need it. Insurance companies attempt to figure out a person's risk of getting sick and price insurance higher for these people. Thus an older person who does not have health insurance on the job may find it impossible to buy insurance. Although some people may find this morally reprehensible, this is not a problem of moral hazard; this is simply a problem of someone whose income is too low to afford to buy the goods she wants. This is not a market failure in the traditional sense, and the justification for government intervention to solve this problem must rely on an equity argument.

Market Failure and Government Failure

The notion that government can promote efficiency has frequently been criticized. This chapter has laid out examples of market failures and presented ways that the government could address those failures, as if the government was a perfectly working institution. It is incorrect to assume that the market always works efficiently, but it also is incorrect to assume that the government always works efficiently. Prudent government

Chapter Six

Cost-Benefit and Cost-Effectiveness Analysis

To be worth doing, any government action justified by market failure must prove to be a Pareto improvement. Cost-benefit analysis (using the rule for optimal decision making from chapter 2) is one method used to assess whether a government program results in a Pareto improvement.

The second broad justification for government intervention in the marketplace, to change the distribution of property, does not rely on the concept of market failure and does not require that programs result in Pareto improvement. Cost-benefit analysis also can be useful for assessing programs using the distributional justification, but the costs and benefits must be specified differently. If the efficiency justification is used, the government must compare both the benefits and costs to society as a whole and should take only those actions that improve society as a whole. If it uses the distributional justification, the government specifies costs in the same way but must specify the benefits in terms of some normative criteria for a desirable distribution of property.

Distributional and efficiency justifications for government action are often confused in policy debates, but economists insist on a strict separation. If the poor cannot afford housing, the housing market has not failed; if the poor cannot afford health care, the health-care market has not failed. These are distributional problems that require an equity justification, and economists recommend dealing with distributional issues on their own terms. Distributional issues are considered in later chapters. This chapter focuses on using cost-benefit analysis to assess efficiency improvements.

The Purpose of Cost-Benefit Analysis

Cost-benefit analysis extends the tools of optimal decision making, discussed in chapter 2, to government decision making. Any social policy—just like any other economic action—uses resources and makes them unavailable for other uses. In other words, to obtain a desired outcome society must forgo the opportunity to obtain some other outcome. Using the optimal decision-making rule, a policy is worth implementing only if it is more desirable than any other outcome that could have been obtained by using those resources. Cost-benefit analysis simply compares the estimated social benefit of a policy to the estimated social cost (in an opportunity cost sense) of that policy. The social opportunity cost is the value of the wants forgone as a result of allocating resources to the implementation of this policy. Both the benefits and costs are valued in monetary units. The difference between the social benefit and social cost of a policy is the net benefit. If the net benefit of a policy is positive, the policy improves efficiency, but if it is negative, the policy is not improving efficiency.[1]

Using the criterion of Pareto efficiency with social costs and social benefits creates a problem: Different people often enjoy the benefits and bear the costs. Ensuring that not even one person is made worse off by a policy change is difficult, if not impossible. If the Pareto efficiency criterion were applied strictly, the government would implement few, if any, policies because even policies that would make great improvements for the average person could leave a few people monetarily worse off. To get around this problem economists have invented the compensation test. According to the **compensation test,** or **compensation criterion,** a policy improves efficiency if those who gain from the policy could compensate those who lose so that, after compensation, no one would be a loser. Thus the policy in question ought to be put into effect. The compensation test does not require that such compensation actually be paid; it merely requires the possibility of it.

For example, suppose a policy generated benefits for one group that totaled $2 million and costs to another group that totaled $1 million. In principle the gainers could get together, transfer $1 million to the losers, and still have $1 million left. If such compensation were made, no one would lose as a result of the policy. Even if compensation is not paid, the benefits to society were larger than the costs to society, even though they were enjoyed and borne by different people. Using the compensation test, any program with a greater social benefit than social cost improves efficiency and thus is worth doing from the perspective of society as a whole. In the next section we use an extended example to demonstrate how cost-benefit analysis is applied. Note that this is a purely hypothetical example and that the figures used are not drawn from real data and may have no relationship to actual figures.

Measuring the Net Benefits of the Teen Drinking Program

Suppose Dana Brown, a public policy analyst, heads a committee of economists and social workers who are studying the social effects of teenage drinking. The social workers find that teen drinking is highly correlated with adult alcoholism, drunk driving, and many health problems. The economists on the committee are impressed that these correlated effects are socially costly (for example, the mortality and health cost of accidents caused by drunk driving). Therefore, some government action to curtail teen drinking might improve efficiency, but this does not mean that any policy aimed at reducing teen drinking will increase efficiency.

Suppose Congress is considering a bill that would require secondary schools to hire social workers with expertise in teen alcohol abuse to run groups with teens, and it has hired Brown to conduct a cost-benefit analysis of this policy. For simplicity, assume that Brown has been asked to compare the social costs and benefits of the policy of having social workers run groups to educate teens about the dangers of drinking. The net benefit of employing the social workers is the difference between the social benefit of this program and the social cost of this program. Assume (for simplicity) that the labor of social workers is the only input required to produce the reduction in alcohol consumption among teens and that secondary schools would need to hire five thousand additional social workers to make the program possible.

The social benefit of the teen program is the decrease in health-care costs associated with drinking that can be attributed to this program, the decrease in deaths resulting from drunk driving, and the decrease in psychic costs associated with alcohol abuse. First, Brown will have to find some way to estimate the effect of the teen program on these variables and then estimate the monetary value of these changes. Perhaps the most difficult step in this process would be assessing the relationship between the social workers' actions and teen drinking. However, this assessment is generally considered to be the realm of social workers and health-care analysts rather than economists. For simplicity, assume that social workers have already estimated the effects of social workers on teen drinking and the problems that go along with it. For the rest of the chapter the focus is on the area in which economists are more familiar, assessing the monetary value of the relevant variables.

Suppose that by reducing teen alcohol consumption, the teen program would reduce by $50 million the amount spent on teen health problems related to drinking and would cut by fifteen hundred the number of deaths related to teen drunk driving. How can Brown measure the value of fifteen hundred human lives in monetary terms? This is one of the most difficult and controversial questions that the cost-benefit analyst must confront, but Brown could draw upon the tools of revealed preference to obtain an estimate of the value of human life by using the labor market data approach. The **labor market data approach** is a method of valuing human lives that relies on data on the trade-offs that workers make between higher and lower wages and between a higher and lower risk of death on the job. Some may balk at putting a price on human life. We will discuss this issue shortly, but readers understand that the value of a human life presented here is meant only to represent how much individuals with limited resources would spend to protect their lives from risks when they have other valid concerns, such as providing for a good quality of life for themselves and their family.

Data on how likely workers are to be killed in various jobs and the wage rates associated with these jobs are widely available.[2] The amount of increase in wages that workers are willing to accept in exchange for an increased chance of death on the job reveals the monetary value that workers put on their own lives. This value is the minimum amount of money that workers are willing to accept to face a higher risk of death and the maximum they are willing to give up to face a lower risk. The value of human life is calculated by the following formula:

$$\text{Value of human life} = \text{Money} \div \text{probability}[3]$$

"Money" stands for the maximum amount of money that workers are willing to give up to decrease their risk of death and the minimum they are willing to accept for an increased risk; "probability" stands for the increase or decrease in the probability that a worker will be killed on the job.[4] Suppose statistical studies show that workers, on average, are willing to accept an additional $60 per year in wages to take a job that increases their risk of dying to 2 deaths for every 100,000 workers. Using the formula, the value of human life becomes

$$\text{Value of human life} = \$60 \div (2/100{,}000) = \$3{,}000{,}000$$

Brown calculates the lifesaving value of the policy by multiplying the decrease in deaths by the estimated value of a human life:

$$1{,}500 \times \$3{,}000{,}000 = \$4{,}500{,}000{,}000$$

Adding the $50 million savings in health-care costs gives $4.55 billion for the monetary value of the benefit of the teen alcohol program for one year.

This calculation leaves out the reduction in psychic costs caused by alcohol abuse. Such costs include the anguish felt by relatives of alcoholics, relatives of the victims of drunk-driving accidents, and other examples of negative externalities. These costs are extremely hard to measure because there is no market for pain and suffering. Examining awards in lawsuits for pain and suffering might provide an idea of how much money jurors believe pain and suffering are worth, but trying to turn that into a general principle would be difficult. Analysts often simply ignore these costs. Another way of dealing with them is to discuss them in the written report of the findings of the cost-benefit analysis, paying particular attention to how including them, if this were possible, might affect the conclusions of the analysis.

Once Brown has calculated the benefits, she will need to calculate the costs. If the market for social workers were perfectly competitive and in long-run equilibrium, the opportunity cost of a given social worker would equal the wage of that worker. A simple comparison of the assumptions of perfect competition to the market for social workers will demonstrate that this market is not competitive. However, to make their job easier economists often assume that markets for factors of production are perfectly competitive anyway. Thus Brown could obtain the total cost of the teen alcohol policy by multiplying the wage of social workers by the number of social workers required for the program. This would make the calculations very simple. Suppose the wage of a social worker is $40,000 a year. The total cost of hiring five thousand social workers for one year is $200 million. For a program with benefits of $4.55 billion, this cost is quite small and the compensation criterion is easily satisfied. However, if Brown takes into account the lack of a perfectly competitive market for social workers, the results may not be the same.

The government is not a small firm in a large market for social workers. In fact, it is probably, by far, the largest employer of social workers, and the monopsony model (described in chapter 4) is more appropriate. Employees in a monopsonistic market are paid less than the value of what they produce. Their wages do not reflect the value of what is given up by reallocating the money to some other endeavor. Instead of using their wages, Brown has to estimate the value of what these five thousand social workers would otherwise be producing if they were not employed in a teen alcohol program. For example, suppose that to supply five thousand social workers to the teen alcohol program, the government would have to reassign them from working on projects to curtail domestic violence.[5] The cost of the teen alcohol policy, then, is the value of the reduction in cases of domestic violence that must be forgone in order to assign social workers to the reduction of teenage drinking.

To measure the opportunity cost of five thousand social workers, Brown will have to estimate the health-care costs, the costs in terms of lost life, and the psychic costs of the suffering caused by domestic violence. Then she will have to estimate how much these costs would increase if social workers were reassigned from domestic violence to teenage drinking. Victims of domestic violence are often injured as a result of attacks, requiring costly treatment. Thus, if domestic violence rises because fewer social workers are working to prevent domestic violence, the health-care costs to the victims of domestic violence will increase.

Suppose Brown estimates that a reallocation of five thousand social workers would increase the health-care costs of treating victims of domestic violence by $250 million per year and that the number of deaths from domestic violence would increase by one thousand. Multiplying the number of increased deaths by the value of human life gives the monetary value for the lives lost by reallocating social workers:

$$1,000 \times \$3,000,000 = \$3,000,000,000$$

Adding this to the health-care costs of $250 million gives a figure of $3.25 billion per year as the total cost of allocating five thousand social workers to the curtailment of teen drinking instead of domestic violence.

As with teen drinking, this assessment of the costs leaves out the psychic costs felt by the victims and families of the victims of domestic violence. If the psychic costs were exactly the same for each of these two social problems, the calculation of the relative value of funds spent on one or the other would be unaffected, but it is by no means certain that these costs do balance out. However, even if the psychic costs are not the same, to change the answer they would have to be unbalanced enough to justify the reallocation of social workers. Whether psychic costs can be safely ignored is left to readers' judgment.

The psychic costs aside, the social benefit of the teen alcohol program is $4.55 billion, and the opportunity cost is $3.25 billion. The net benefit of the teen alcohol program is therefore $1.3 billion ($4.55 billion − $3.25 billion = $1.3 billion). Brown therefore advises the government to implement the teen alcohol policy.

Criticism of Cost-Benefit Analysis

One criticism of cost-benefit analysis can be directed at the Pareto improvement criterion itself, because it grounds the compensation test, the basis for cost-benefit analysis. The Pareto criterion is different from that typically used by social workers. Social workers tend to judge the desirability of social policies by whether they are fair and meet people's needs. This, of course, raises the complicated philosophical problem of what humans' needs are. The Pareto improvement criterion judges "better off" and "worse off" by referring to people's wants without considering the possibility that people might want what is bad for them and not want what is good for them. It neglects the possibility that a policy that causes at least one person to gain more of what he wants, without anyone else losing something she wants, would still be a bad policy if what is gained is bad for the person who gains it. Although the idea that people might want what is bad for them is anathema to many economists, it probably is not to many social workers, given their experiences in working with children and mentally incompetent adults (e.g., developmentally disabled and mentally ill adults). Economists would probably respond that rational choice theory was not developed for application to children and the mentally ill, although, as we stated in chapter 1, it could be applied to people with strange preferences. Economists are not clamoring to eliminate mental institutions. Among competent adults, however, most economists would probably say that only two methods exist to judge an individual's needs and wants: Either the individual can judge her own needs, or someone can judge for her. If the individual is competent, the benefit of the doubt should go to the individual.

Another criticism that can be made directly against the compensation criterion is that it pays no attention to who receives the benefits and who pays the costs. As long as the gainers gain more than the losers, the compensation principle says that the government should enact the policy, regardless of whether the gainers are already relatively wealthy and the losers are relatively poor or vice versa. Social workers probably would not care as much about the efficiency aspects of a policy as they would about its equity or fairness aspects. They probably would wonder why society should enact a policy that would lead the already well-off to gain and the already bad-off to lose, even if the gains improve efficiency. Some economists have developed a technique to address such concerns. They advocate the use of what are called distributional weights.

The compensation test assumes that a dollar is worth the same to everyone, regardless of income. Distributional weights are essentially a handicapping system that assumes that an additional dollar is more valuable to someone with a small income than to someone with a large income. Many economists would object to this criterion because it makes an **interpersonal comparison of utility**—it compares the satisfaction that different people receive from a change in the allocation of resources. That is, who is to say that a dollar means less to someone with more income? However, on this basis the compensation principle does not work, either, because who is to say that a dollar means the same to a millionaire as it does to a poor person?

Distributional weights are a way to systematically adjust the costs and benefits of policies in order to take equity into account. For example, suppose a program would provide a social benefit of $4 billion, incur an opportunity cost of $3 billion, and would primarily benefit upper-middle-class people. The majority of those who would bear the cost of the program are poor. The net benefit of this program would be $1 billion; according to the compensation criterion, the program would improve efficiency and therefore would be worth doing. But suppose the analyst assumes that a dollar is worth only one-fifth as much to upper-middle-class people as it is to poor people. Thus the distributional weights are 0.2 for a wealthier individual and 1.00 for a poor person. The following formula takes distributional weights into account in the cost-benefit analysis:

$$(0.2 \times \$4 \text{ billion}) - (1 \times \$3 \text{ billion}) = \$0.8 \text{ billion}$$
$$- \$3 \text{ billion} = -\$2.2 \text{ billion}$$

Taking into account these distributional weights reveals a net loss of $2.2 billion instead of a net gain of $3 billion. Thus, while cost-benefit analysis using the compensation principle implies that the policy should be enacted, the distributional weights imply that it should not. The problem with using distributional weights is that there is no clear way to determine what they should be. Had the distributional weights been 0.8 and 1 instead of 0.2 and 1, the calculation would have resulted in a net gain of $0.2 billion. A critic of the use of distributional weights in cost-benefit analysis could argue that using any weights amounts to the government's favoring one group over another. Of course, those who think that government should favor some groups over others would not see a problem with the approach. This is still an unsettled issue.

Economists would probably respond that questions about the equity of the distribution of income should be settled separately from problems of efficiency. If the distribution of income is unfair, to correct the distribution of income society should use the policy that causes the fewest disruptions to efficiency so that it can set this issue aside when considering the efficiency ramifications of every other policy.

One of the most impassioned criticisms of cost-benefit analysis challenges the moral legitimacy of the attempt to place a monetary value on human life. The social analyst Steven Kelman argues that humans think that some things are appropriately valued in monetary terms—inanimate objects such as cars, trucks, shoes, and the like—but other things are priceless.[6] That is, some things—such as human life—are so valuable that to put a monetary price tag on them would amount to a lack of appreciation for how valuable they really are. In other words, any monetary price tag on the value of human life underestimates its true value and distorts the assessments of the true social costs and benefits of any action that risks a human life.

Perhaps most social workers will find Kelman's critique compelling, but economists have responses that cannot easily be dismissed. As they see it, the value or worth of something has to do with how much satisfaction or utility a person derives from consuming it. And how much utility a person derives from something is measured by how much of something else that person is willing to give up to obtain it. This principle can be applied to life as well as any other good. Devoting resources to living longer involves trading off resources that could be used to make life more enjoyable, and an action that increases a person's lifespan is worth taking only if the marginal increase in lifespan is more valuable than the marginal decrease in consumption of other goods.

We need not look at people who take unnecessary risks—like smoking cigarettes and eating fatty foods—to see economists' point; we need only consider the everyday risks that everyone accepts almost without thinking about them. Have you ever driven a car? If you really believed life was priceless, you wouldn't, because you know that every time you step into a car, no matter how good a driver you are, a small chance exists that you will get into a fatal accident. If you limited yourself to walking and using public transportation, your life expectancy would increase. Would it be worth it? The answer to that question involves placing a value on human life.

What would a society look like that really believed life was priceless? It would have no automobiles, no airplanes, and no trains, or perhaps it would have trains that moved at three miles per hour to make it extremely unlikely that they could ever have a fatal accident. But a society that believed life was priceless also would have no television, no sports, no art, and no flowers. It would spend no money on any activity that did not save lives because limited resources means that every dollar spent on nonlifesaving activities is a dollar not spent on lifesaving activities such as medical research. If we, as a society, allocated our entire gross domestic product to essential food, essential shelter, and essential education and left all the rest for medical research, we would save lives. But even this many resources would not eliminate all premature deaths. Thus, if we truly believed life is priceless, we would spend all our time and all our money on lifesaving activities, and we would have nothing left for other types of activities. Do you think you would enjoy living in a society that devoted itself entirely to producing necessities and conducting medical research? Probably not, and an economist would say that if you have ever spent a dollar on something that didn't directly preserve life, by revealed preference you have demonstrated that life is not priceless to you.

Economists would say that some trade-off between quantity of life and quality of life must exist. But once you have taken this step, you have tacitly put a price on life. Economists would say that such tacit trade-offs could be better made if they are made explicitly. So long as scarcity forces society to put a value on life, society should try to make that decision rationally by assessing the value of life as accurately as possible. Note that putting a value on human life, even as small as $3 million, often implies that the government should devote far more resources to preserving human life than it does. Studies of the value of medical research based on a monetary value of human life have shown that such research is underfunded by billions of dollars. For example, if it takes ten social workers to save only one life per year, the marginal benefit of each social worker (and thus the amount society could afford to pay social workers) is $300,000 a year. This hypothesis also implies that if the going wage for social workers is far less, the government could afford to hire many more social workers until the law of diminishing returns causes their marginal benefit to drop down to their wage.

Other critics of cost-benefit analysis do not object in principle to putting a price on human life but instead raise questions about the way economists typically measure the value of human life. Remember that the value of human life was calculated using the labor market data, which assume—unrealistically—that workers know the risks of dying associated with various occupations. If workers are not aware of the death risks associated with various occupations, assuming that workers are knowingly placing monetary values on their lives is unreasonable. Thus, even if putting a value on human life is acceptable, using labor market data to value human life is questionable.

An alternative to using labor market data is the **lifetime earnings approach,** a method of valuing human life that relies on predictions of how much money a worker is likely to make during her or his lifetime.[7] Statistical methods can be used to predict workers' lifetime earnings. Although this method uses average earnings simply as a guide to the value of an average person, this approach implies that the sole value of a human life is the money a person makes and that people who make more money are more valuable workers and are more valuable human beings. Social workers are likely to find these assumptions distasteful.

Cost-Effectiveness Analysis

Some analysts have used cost-effectiveness analysis as an efficiency criterion that allows analysts to evaluate public policies with life-and-death consequences without putting an explicit monetary value on human life. The measurement of opportunity cost is no different in cost-effectiveness analysis. The main difference between the two is that cost-effectiveness analysis does not value benefits in monetary terms. Instead they are quantified in some other way, depending upon the nature of the policy or program being assessed. The cost-effectiveness analyst computes a cost-effectiveness (CE) ratio between two comparison programs. The CE ratio compares the costs of a program to its effectiveness, which does not have to be calculated in dollars.[8]

Suppose Eric Black is a social worker who conducts research on the effectiveness of social work counseling services provided to heroin addicts. Black has the opportunity to do research in a New York agency that uses two different treatment approaches: the Freudian approach and the behavioral approach. He takes a random sample of heroin-addicted clients and randomly assigns twenty to receive Freudian treatment (the F group) and twenty to receive behavioral treatment (the B group). The outcome measure is the number of those in each group who enter a detoxification program at some point during a two-year period *after* receiving treatment. Entering a detoxification program subsequent to treatment would be a sign that the treatment has failed.

Assume, for the sake of simplicity, that the only inputs used by both approaches are the services of social workers, all of whom are paid $40,000 per year. Suppose the behavioral approach requires five social workers and the Freudian approach requires ten social workers, because social workers must spend more time with each client. The total cost of the behavioral approach is $200,000 per year ($40,000 × 5), and the total cost of the Freudian approach is $400,000 ($40,000 × 10). Black would use these figures as his measures of relative program costs.

Black decides to use the reduction in the number of admissions to detoxification programs as his measure of relative program effectiveness. Two years after treatment, five out of the twenty exposed to the Freudian approach had entered a detoxification program at some point during the observation period, and the same was true for ten of the twenty exposed to the behavioral approach. Thus the Freudian approach averted fifteen admissions, while the behavioral approach averted ten.

Black computes the CE ratio for his study. The social cost of the Freudian approach is $200,000 ($400,000 − $200,000) and its social effectiveness is 5 admissions averted (15 − 10). The CE ratio is

$$\$200,000 \div 5 = \$40,000$$

This value for the CE ratio means that by moving from using a behavioral to a Freudian approach to treating heroin addiction, social costs increase by $40,000 per additional admission averted. Upon becoming aware of Black's findings, those responsible for making decisions about allocating societal resources would have to decide whether they are willing to pay $40,000 for each additional admission averted.

If Brown applied this same method to her comparison of using five thousand social workers for the teen alcohol program or using them for domestic violence services, she would find that the cost of the social workers is the same whether they work in domestic violence or in the teen alcohol program but that they can avert one thousand deaths from domestic violence or fifteen hundred deaths from drunk driving. Thus society would be able to save additional lives without increasing social costs.

One difficulty of cost-effectiveness analysis is that it cannot compare different kinds of outcomes. Using deaths as the measure of the effectiveness of the teen alcohol and domestic violence programs requires ignoring the health-care costs. In this example, the health costs were insignificant compared to the cost in human lives. But this will not always be the case. Programs often have a number of different effects of different sizes that need to be measured together to come up with an overall measure of effectiveness. Economists use monetary value as a yardstick for estimating the relative values of very different effects.

This chapter and chapter 5 are both concerned with what policies the government ought to enact, although each chapter addresses this question from a slightly different perspective. The next chapter changes course. Instead of examining theory about what government should do, it examines a theory of what government actually does.

Chapter Seven

Government Failure

Like market failures, government failures are possible. Although the discussion thus far has assumed that government is a benign entity that would act to rectify market failures, economists since Adam Smith have pointed out that there is no certainty that a government, even a democratic one, will choose the efficient policy responses to market failures, even if economists could identify efficient policies.[1]

Beginning in the 1950s and 1960s, a group of economists, who have come to be called public choice theorists, began to address government failures by using mainstream economic tools.[2] More specifically, their method was to apply to political decision making the same rational choice tools that economists apply to marketplace decision making. Public choice theory assumes that people vote, pass legislation, run for office, give campaign contributions, or lobby Congress to maximize their own private benefit (whether it be utility or profit).

From the perspective of rational choice theory the difference between public sector institutions and profit-seeking firms is important. A company's objective is fairly clear: to make profits. Even if a corporation has thousands of stockholders, it is reasonable to believe that they are all united in their desire for the firm to make as much money as possible. Governments, on the other hand, do not have owners and do not directly make profits, yet every action that a government takes affects the income of firms and individuals throughout the country. Often, government policy makes some people better off and others worse off. For example, the federal government taxes middle-class people not to make a profit but to finance programs that benefit the poor or perhaps another segment of the middle class. One central feature of democratic decision making is the existence of groups with opposing interests that may seek social policies to serve themselves, perhaps at the expense of others. Public choice theorists therefore do not speak of the government's goal as they would speak of the firm's goal, but to come up with a theory of government they consider the competing goals of different actors in the political decision-making process.

Because public choice theory is concerned with government failure, many of its practitioners are rather pessimistic about government, and they tend to be advocates of "small government." But it would be wrong to view public choice as simply a rationalization for small government. The theory is well thought out. Building a good government requires a good understanding of what can go wrong with government. Public choice theory offers important insights about the workings of modern governments.

Rent Seeking

Ideally, the goal of government policies is to make everyone better off, but the individuals who make and influence policy may be interested in rent seeking. Remember that (economic) *rent* is another word for *profit*, particularly profit that is either unearned or higher than the normal rate of return on investment. The government's power to regulate, tax, and subsidize markets and the large amount of buying and selling it does give it the ability to create a lot of rent for individuals and firms. **Rent seeking** is the pursuit of private profit through the political process. Lobbyists and interest groups are the prime suspects in rent seeking, but politicians, bureaucrats, and voters may get in on it as well.

You might think that the profit that a firm makes from government policies would be an insignificant by-product of policy designed to increase social welfare, but the profits rather than the social benefit or costs may be what drive policymaking. A policy that increases the benefit for society as a whole benefits every individual a little bit, but a policy that creates rents benefits one small group a whole lot. A large group that benefits little does not have much incentive to press hard for political action, but a small group that sees a rent-seeking opportunity has a great incentive to pressure the government a lot. Therefore, a large amount of what the government does may be influenced more by rent seeking than by genuine concern for social benefits.

The relationship between imperfect competition and rent seeking is important. Chapter 4 stated that monopoly is inefficient because a monopoly produces a suboptimal level of output, but this does not count the effort that a monopoly makes to gain and protect its monopoly status. Government regulations are a large source (perhaps the primary source) of market power and thus of rent, which is why companies spend billions of dollars to hire lobbyists to obtain favorable regulations from the government. **Rent avoidance** occurs when other firms spend billions more to discourage the government from passing regulations that favor their opponents. The resources allocated to these activities could have been allocated to the actual production of goods, and therefore the time and effort spent on rent seeking must be considered a social cost.

Examples of rent seeking are not hard to find. For example, most of the logging conducted in the United States is done on government-owned land. The government allows firms to use this land for low fees and often builds roads through national forestland at taxpayers' expense to make the area more accessible to logging firms. Legislators often justify such policy as a way to boost the economy, but public choice economists suspect they do it because of the campaign contributions they get from logging companies. Other examples—and they are many—include farm price supports, which make food more expensive for everyone but benefit farmers. Tariffs help local producers but hurt consumers. Government tax policy favors the small number of people whose income comes largely from capital gains, not the large number of people whose income comes from wages or salaries. The list is almost endless, but another example may cut a little too close to home.

At this writing New York was considering a social work–licensing bill. If this bill becomes law, individuals would be required to be licensed before they could legitimately practice social work, and only those with certain academic credentials would be eligible for licensing. Social workers were lobbying vigorously for passage of this bill. They would probably say that they support this bill to ensure that clients receive high-quality services, but a public choice theorist would view such an explanation skeptically. If the licensing bill were passed, the supply of social workers would decrease, increasing the income of the remaining social workers (see fig. 3.7), because purchasers of social work services would have fewer social workers to choose from. Other health professionals are allocating resources to block passage of the bill. The public choice theorist would probably view these as textbook examples of rent seeking and rent avoidance and would see a good deal of waste in all this. The time of social workers, other health professionals, and professional lobbyists could be used to provide other services if it weren't going into lobbying.[3]

Some readers might take offense at public choice theorists' suggestion that they are seeking to benefit themselves at the expense of others. However, public choice theorists do not believe that social workers are the only ones who engage in rent seeking. Were you ready to believe that logging companies, farmers, and financiers were willing to engage in rent seeking? Then, why not social workers?

Rent seeking would never succeed if it weren't for legislators' willingness to pass legislation sought by rent seekers. Why would legislators be willing to do this? Aren't they supposed to enact only legislation that is in the "public interest"? Perhaps they are supposed to, but this is rarely what they actually do. Legislators are mainly interested in gaining and remaining in office. Because they ultimately gain and remain in office only by getting more votes than their opponents, they are interested in supporting legislation that they think will get them votes or campaign contributions, regardless of whether the legislation is efficient or in the public interest. Some economists believe that the government could run almost entirely on rent seeking. If rent-seeking special interest groups could form a coalition that represents 51 percent of the voting population, all government policies might be directly related to redistributing income to the 51 percent in power.

Noneconomists usually say that the solution to rent seeking is to elect people who care about the public interest. But economists then point out that selfish people can pretend that they are concerned with the public interest just to get the job and then immediately start rent seeking, or they may find that pandering to rent seekers is a more effective way of getting the job than promoting broad social interests. Economists look for a mechanism that will cause public policy to reflect the general interest, despite its being set and carried out by people acting in their own self-interest. Does an invisible hand cause political outcomes to be efficient? Or, if not, can we create a set of rules for government behavior that will minimize opportunities for rent seeking? This is called the problem of mechanism design.

Mechanism design is the search for a constitution that will result in social policies that generate Pareto improvements, even though the policies are enacted and implemented only by people who are interested in rent seeking. The U.S. system of checks and balances that divides power between the president, Congress, and the courts is one attempt to design a mechanism that will serve the public interest, but it is far from perfect.

A host of economists from Adam Smith to modern public choice theorists have advocated limiting government functions to the fewest activities possible in order to limit opportunities for self-serving political action. But we could argue that when opportunities for efficiency-improving or social justice–improving actions exist, government inaction is itself a form of government failure. Arguing to limit government activity itself may be a form of rent seeking by those who would benefit from lower taxes, regardless of whether low tax policies are best for society as a whole. There's no easy answer. We will always need government, but like markets, it will always be prone to failure.

Bureaucracy

Social workers often complain about bureaucracies, especially that bureaucrats are unresponsive to the requests of social workers and their clients. Another, related complaint is that bureaucracies are too big. Another is that government has too many divisions or departments, many of which appear to be unnecessary. What social worker has not spent large amounts of time on the phone being transferred from one division to another without any being helpful? Public choice theorists' views on bureaucracy should be of interest to a profession that has such intimate contact with this type of administrative structure.

The market failures discussed in chapter 5 notwithstanding, one major advantage of markets is that they put pressure on employees of competitive for-profit firms to be responsive to consumers. Employees who are not responsive do not keep their jobs long because their firms lose customers to those with more responsive employees. Employees in public sector bureaucracies do not face the same incentive to be responsive to the public. Government bureaucracies usually do not have competition, and a government bureaucrat's job and salary are typically fairly secure and do not vary much, if at all, with her day-to-day activities. For example, civil service laws, not levels of productivity or responsiveness to clients' concerns, largely govern the positions and salaries of child welfare workers.

Competitive pressure forces a firm's manager or employee to maximize profit, but how does the manager or employee of a bureaucracy behave when his job and income are relatively secure and competitive pressure does not exist? If there is no profit to maximize, the rational agent will maximize utility. Most economists conclude that employees in such circumstances will want to shirk or work as little as possible. This belief seems to be substantiated by common complaints from social workers, and others, that bureaucrats do not work very hard and seldom stay in the office past 5:01 P.M. None of this is to say that all government bureaucrats are lazy but just to point out that employees in large bureaucracies have little incentive to behave as diligently as those in competitive firms. We should also note that economists have recognized that employees in large public bureaucracies share some problems with those in large private for-profit bureaucracies, especially those that are under relatively less competitive pressure.

Managers of bureaucracies might derive utility from running large agencies, which may make them feel like big shots. Managers also may have more information than legislators do about how many resources are necessary to accomplish the goals of their agencies; this may give the managers an opportunity to mislead legislators about how many resources their agencies need. As a result, government bureaucracies would tend to become huge organizations with superfluous employees who have little incentive to be responsive to the concerns of clients or consumers. This, of course, is exactly the situation that many critics say already exists.

Legislators may get wise to this process and discount bureaucrats' claims of how much money they need to accomplish a given task. However, bureaucrats can respond by further exaggerating their needs or canceling one of the most politically popular functions of their department to prove that they really need the money to keep operating. City child welfare managers might cancel a special division to protect children neglected by drug-addicted parents in order to prove that the agency needs the money that was cut. The solution might be for legislators to appoint unselfish civic-minded people to run bureaucracies, but selfish people are good at pretending to be unselfish people if they can benefit from doing so. Another solution could be to try to limit the scope of bureaucracy and replace bureaucracies with competitive firms, but bureaucracies exist for a reason: to provide services not easily provided by the market. Thus so long as we need bureaucracies, we will need to find a way to make them run more efficiently.

Rational Nonvoting

Especially in election years, the op-ed pages of newspapers are full of discussions of why more people do not vote. Some critics believe that apathy or cynicism must be at epidemic levels, because so few people care enough about the important political issues to vote. Economists, however, are concerned with exactly the opposite question: Why does anyone vote? In a large democracy any individual's vote is statistically meaningless. The odds against any election's being decided by just one vote are astronomical. Take your one vote away from the winning side or add one vote to the losing side and there is no effect on the outcome. Yet voting has a cost. Voters have to go to the polls, wait in line, and lose time that they could use to do something else with a more obvious payoff. When someone compares the real loss in time that voting takes to the far-fetched possibility that her single vote will affect the outcome, the rational response would seem to be not to waste time voting. Thus economists conclude that all those people who do not vote are perfectly rational.

What about all those people who do vote? Are they irrational? If so, that challenges economists' assumption that people are rational. This theoretical predicament has several ways out, but none is completely satisfying. One idea is that as fewer people vote, the likelihood that one vote could be decisive increases, which would give rational people more of an incentive to vote. However, except for a few elections in small jurisdictions, this is not likely to occur. The likelihood that one person's vote will be decisive is small, and this perspective does not explain why people are more likely to vote in national rather than local elections. That is, people are *most* likely to vote in elections where their vote is *least* likely to be decisive.

However, so many people fail to vote that voter turnout, instead of a particular individual's vote, is a significant factor in elections. Perhaps voting reflects a tacit agreement among people of a certain belief that all will vote if all the others will. This explanation is dissatisfying to economists, however, because individuals would have an incentive to break any such agreement. If everyone in my coalition votes, my vote is unnecessary, and if no one in my coalition votes, my vote would not help.

Perhaps people get satisfaction from voting. They may vote because doing so allows them to feel good about being part of "the team" (if they voted for the winner) or carrying out their civic duty. This explanation is not completely satisfying to most economists, either, but sociologists and sociologically minded economists might find it appealing. Sociologists believe that people are members of communities that possess social norms, rules about how people should and should not behave, and that some significant proportion of members of a given community is committed to enforcing those norms. Some older members of these communities teach younger ones the community's norms, causing younger members to internalize them. In the language of economics internalization of social norms affects the learners' wants so that they want to do what the norms prescribe. Members of the U.S. community are taught that they have a civic duty to vote. Perhaps this has resulted in our internalizing such notions, which may explain why we vote when rational choice theory predicts that we will not.

Social workers might wonder why they should care about why people do or do not vote. The answer is simple. The National Association of Social Workers' code of ethics states that social workers have a professional obligation to get involved and attempt to get other citizens involved in efforts to enact more socially just policies. One of the main ways that social workers and others affect social policies, just or otherwise, is through voting. Thus, if social workers take this professional obligation seriously, it behooves them to try to figure out why people do or do not vote so they can better understand how to get more people to do it.

Voting, of course, is not the only way that people can influence social policy. They can lobby their representatives, organize other members of their community to do so, participate in demonstrations, or engage in an armed insurrection or a host of other activities. Some predictions about nonvoting could be made about other forms of political participation, unless they are more likely to have some tangible payoff. For example, Jamie was a community organizer in a poor area of Brooklyn, New York.

She worked for an organization that advocated universal health care and attempted to get neighborhood residents to participate in a demonstration for such a system. Most of the people she encouraged to participate did not do so. Many of these nonparticipants voiced support for universal health care and clearly felt that they would benefit from such a plan. Yet they still chose not to take part in an effort to bring it about. Why? The public choice economist has a ready answer.

If universal health care became a reality, all those who wanted to see this policy enacted would derive satisfaction from its existence, whether they took part in demonstrations or other actions to help bring it about or not. In other words, in the language of chapter 5 universal health care would be a public good. Thus those who want to see such a policy enacted would have an incentive to wait for others to work to bring it about and free-ride on their accomplishment if they succeed.

Some of the residents whom Jamie encouraged to participate in the demonstration did so. Why didn't they choose to free-ride? This question should be of interest to social workers, at least those inclined toward community mobilization. Once again, sociology might provide part of the answer. Perhaps those who chose to participate in these demonstrations were socialized in such a way that they derive utility from taking part in activist pursuits. Standard economic theory with a sociological spin also offers an explanation. Perhaps those who participated in these demonstrations obtained private goods or benefits that only those who took part were able to obtain. Perhaps they obtained more status in their community, derived utility from defying authority, or derived utility from knowing that they were directly involved in making a difference in their world. Or maybe they like hanging out with the type of people who usually go to demonstrations. Such private goods, plus the anticipated public good of universal health care, might have been enough to outweigh the cost of participating in demonstrations, offsetting the free-rider problem. Thus making political participation directly beneficial to the participants themselves could lead to greater involvement.

Those who wish to make good social policy should not ignore the problems discussed in this chapter, but they are not easy to solve. It is hoped that mechanisms can be designed to keep these problems to a minimum, but it is unlikely that they will ever be eliminated. This, of course, does not mean that it is futile to try. Sometimes the most

Chapter Eight

The Economics of Labor

Social workers are acutely aware of the social problems associated with unemployment and low-wage labor, such as domestic violence, low self-esteem, depression, and suicide, and therefore many social workers are interested in proposing various types of policies to address these problems. Policymakers will take such proposals more seriously if those who make them exhibit an understanding of the economic implications of their prescriptions. In this chapter we explore a simple model of an individual's work decision and how this model relates to a supply-and-demand model of the labor market. We also discuss criticism of the supply-and-demand model and the problems of labor market discrimination and unemployment. At several points we touch on how more sociological concerns can be incorporated into the economic approach to analyzing labor markets.

The Labor-Leisure Trade-off

Economists regard the decision to work as a trade-off between labor and leisure in which leisure time is desirable and work is undesirable, except for the money that work pays. But as everyone knows, people do not work simply for money. They work in order to enjoy the companionship of their colleagues, for status, for the intellectual challenges, to avoid being called a lazy shiftless bum, and for a host of reasons other than to make money. Yet economists typically study people's work decisions as if the only reason people work is to get money. Although economists are well aware that people work for nonmonetary reasons, they simply believe that the other reasons for working are irrelevant for building an adequate model of people's work decisions. In other words, if we are interested in developing a model to explain and predict work decisions, the assumption that people work only for money is good enough.

One of the main ways that economists model the work decision is by applying the tools of supply and demand discussed in chapter 3 to an individual's demand for leisure and supply of labor. To understand how this is done you will need to understand what economists mean by "supplying labor" and "demanding leisure." Supplying labor or work is the expenditure of effort, time, knowledge, skills, and the like in exchange for pay. Demanding **leisure** is spending time doing anything that does not make money. Thus telling jokes for fun is demanding leisure; telling jokes for money is supplying labor. Building computers as a hobby is demanding leisure; building computers for money is supplying labor. Taking care of your own children for love is demanding leisure; taking care of someone else's children for money is supplying labor.

Some feminist economists criticize the view that a woman who is taking care of her own children is engaging in leisure, while one who takes care of others' children for a wage is working.[1] This criticism should be directed at people who put a moral judgment on work as something good and somehow better than leisure. Economists, however, do not judge labor as somehow better than leisure but quite the opposite. In economics maximization of efficiency means maximizing the time that people have to do the things they really enjoy (leisure), whether it is raising children or playing basketball, and minimizing the time spent doing things they do not enjoy. Unlike U.S. society as a whole, economic theory does not venerate work as an important social value. In economics labor is a necessary evil (or, more accurately, a necessary disutility) that people must endure to procure the goods they want to consume. Leisure can include some physically demanding activities. The simple thing that separates labor from leisure is that leisure activities are things people do for their own reasons, whereas labor is something people do for money.

Yet other critics might chime in to say that not all people regard labor as a cost or disutility and that the shortcoming of mainstream economics is that it does so. But that discussion is beyond the scope of this book.

Whether people enjoy work or not, they enjoy doing a great many things and have only a limited amount of time to do them. Labor provides the money that people need in order to do the other things they enjoy. Thus an inherent (although not necessarily the only) feature in a person's decision to spend time working or at leisure is the trade-off between the money she will get from work and the enjoyment she will get from leisure. Economists believe that this trade-off captures the most important feature of the labor-leisure choice, and thus they believe that they can focus their model solely on this feature without too much loss of reality. Thus leisure is considered a good that individuals demand, whereas labor is a product that individuals supply (and firms demand).

From the Labor-Leisure Trade-off to the Supply of Labor

The demand for a good depends, among other things, on its price and consumers' incomes. The same is true for leisure. We cannot go to the store to buy leisure in the same way that we can buy social work textbooks, so what could be the meaning of "the price of leisure"? The concept of opportunity cost provides the answer. Recall that the true price or cost of something is always what the buyer must give up to obtain it. What must a person give up to obtain leisure? The answer is the income that person could make at work. Because leisure is whatever a person is doing when he is not working, the cost of leisure is the amount of money he gives up by choosing to spend an hour at leisure instead of at work (or, more technically, the cost of leisure is the goods that this money could buy). What is a person's income when the question is how much leisure to buy? The answer is all of his nonlabor income plus the income he could make if he spent all his available time working.

Assume for simplicity that the most a person could work is one hundred hours per week. If Susan Vega works forty hours a week at $10 per hour, her money income is $400 per week. But she could take a second or a third job and work one hundred hours per week. In that case she would consume little leisure, but she would have an income of $1,000 per week. If she chooses to work only forty hours per week, in an opportunity-cost sense she has spent the first $600 of her potential income on the consumption of leisure.

The supply of labor is the opposite of the demand for leisure. A person who demands sixty hours per week of leisure is therefore supplying forty hours per week of labor. The supply of labor is the relationship between the price of labor (i.e., the wage) and the quantity of labor supplied. As we discussed in chapter 3, we expect the relationship between price and quantity of labor to be positive. That is, the higher the price, the larger the quantity supplied. But this may not be true of labor because the price of labor is closely related to an individual's income, and an individual's income will affect how much leisure he decides to consume.

A change in the price of leisure has two effects that work in opposite directions: the substitution effect and the income effect. The **substitution effect** occurs when a change in the relative price of a good causes a change in the quantity demanded. The **income effect** occurs when a change in income causes a change in demand for some good. A higher wage means that the marginal cost of leisure is higher (a person gives up more money for each hour of leisure); that is, leisure becomes more expensive relative to other goods. Thus people have an incentive to substitute work for leisure (the substitution effect). But a higher wage also means a higher income, so a person has more money with which to purchase all goods, including leisure. Thus a person also has an incentive to purchase more leisure (the income effect). Which of these two effects will be larger is uncertain, so whether an increase in the wage will cause an increase or a decrease in the quantity of labor supplied is uncertain.

For example, suppose Susan's hourly wage increases to $100 an hour from $10 an hour. If she continues to work forty hours, she would make $4,000 per week. She can buy a lot more goods with her income. If Susan were to work one hundred hours, her income would be much higher ($10,000 per week). Because she gives up more goods ($100 per hour instead of $10) by choosing the same amount of leisure, she has an incentive to substitute work for leisure, that is, to work more hours and consume less leisure. But because she has a higher potential income ($10,000), she has an incentive to consume more of all goods, including leisure. The only way to consume more leisure is to supply less labor. Will she work more or less? It depends on her preferences. If the substitution effect is bigger than the income effect, she will work more; if she chooses to work fifty hours per week, she would make $5,000; essentially, she has given up ten hours of leisure for the goods she can buy with an additional $1,000. If the income effect is bigger, she will work less, perhaps working thirty hours and making $3,000 per week. In this case she will have spent $1,000 of her potential income on ten more hours of leisure.

Either outcome is possible, depending on the individual's preferences. Thus it is completely reasonable for someone to respond to an increase in his wage by working less. The uncertain effect of the price of leisure on the consumption of leisure is different from the relationship between the price of other goods and the consumption of them, because the price of leisure is negatively related to income. If the price of strawberries increases, both the substitution effect and the income effect would encourage consumers to buy fewer strawberries. It is unclear whether the labor supply curve has a positive slope like the supply of most goods or whether it is *backward bending*, meaning that as the wage increases, the labor supply increases up to a certain point but then decreases. Some empirical estimates have found that men's work effort is less responsive than women's to changes in wages and social policies that affect wages.[2]

Nonwage income (such as income from investments, welfare benefits, or gifts) correlates positively to the quantity of leisure demanded because a higher nonwage income gives people more purchasing power, which means they can afford more goods, including leisure. This is another instance of the income effect.

The way that economists model labor-leisure decisions allows them to make predictions, some of which are of interest to social workers, about the consequences of various kinds of government policies. Many social policies that social workers care about are partly financed by income taxes. The amount that a person's tax bill changes for each dollar change in income is called the **marginal tax rate**. Changes in marginal tax rates have substitution and income effects just as wage changes do.

For example, suppose that Joe works as a mechanic for a gross wage of $20 per hour, and his current marginal tax rate is 20 percent. So for each dollar increase in his earnings, Joe gets 80 cents, and 20 cents go to the government (0.2 × $1 = 20 cents). Thus for each hour he works, Joe gets $16 and $4 go to the government (0.2 × $20 = $4). If Joe works a forty-hour week for the whole year, his gross income is $41,600; he keeps $33,280 and Uncle Sam gets $8,320.

Now suppose the federal government decides to increase social welfare spending and to finance this by an increase in income taxes that results in Joe's facing a marginal tax rate of 30 percent. Now for each dollar increase in his earnings Joe's tax bill increases by 30 cents. Also, for an hour of work Joe now receives not $16 but $14 (0.3 × $20 = $6 in taxes, which leaves Joe with $14). This still leaves him with annual earnings of

$41,600 if he works forty hours per week, but now he keeps $29,120 and the government gets $12,480. Depending on the size of the income and substitution effects, this could cause either an increase or decrease in the quantity of leisure a person demands (and labor that person supplies). Economic theory does not allow us to determine whether Joe, or those who face similar situations, would supply more or less labor. But it does provide a model of work decisions that allows us to think systematically about the consequences of policies such as these.

Social workers often advocate social policies without giving much thought to how the policies will be financed. An increase in social welfare spending may not do much good if the way it is financed leads to a severe work disincentive that causes a huge number of people to choose not to produce the goods that sustain the society. Also, an increase in social welfare spending might not do much good if the way it is financed leads to such a severe drop in people's incomes that they dramatically increase the hours they spend working just to maintain their living standards.

We are able to speculate about how economic models might be made more complex by incorporating some ideas from sociology. In the United States a norm exists that states that able-bodied people are morally obligated to work for their subsistence. In such a society leisure has a cost beyond forgone earnings. Consider Joe again. As a result of the tax increase, the cost of leisure, measured in forgone earnings, decreases. But if Joe chooses to work less, he still might be called a lazy, immoral, no-good bum by his family, friends, and others whose respect he desires. In other words, what might be called the sociological cost of leisure might not decline as a result of the tax increase. Thus Joe's quantity of leisure demanded might not increase as much as we would think if we considered only the tax increase. In more technical language the failure of the sociological cost to decrease might curtail the substitution effect. Thus an increase in marginal tax rates to finance social welfare programs might not create much of a work disincentive, if the sociological cost of leisure remains constant.[3] An economist would not necessarily have an objection to this analysis; remember that economists do not question how people obtain their preferences but take preferences as given. If, for whatever reason, men prefer to work no less than forty hours per week, economists would just say that the marginal value of leisure drops to zero after men consume sixty hours of leisure per week.

The Demand for Labor

In labor markets companies demand labor and individuals supply it—just the opposite of most markets, where firms are the sellers and individuals are the buyers. However, the labor market is similar in other ways to other markets and is usually modeled by using an adaptation of the perfectly competitive model discussed in chapter 3. This assumes that there are many buyers and sellers of labor who are too small for their decisions to independently affect the market price and that all market participants can enter and leave the market at will.

The demand for labor is a **derived demand,** a demand for a particular factor or product that is dependent on the existence of a demand for some other product; in other words, employers do not demand labor as an end in itself—they demand labor because they believe that those whom they hire will produce a product that will allow the company to make a profit.[4] For example, owners and managers of automobile plants hire workers because the executives and shareholders believe that these workers will produce cars that can be sold for a profit. This is different from a wealthy person who hires a maid because he directly enjoys the services that the maid provides.

Two other concepts are crucial for understanding wage levels: the marginal product and the marginal revenue product. The **marginal product (MP)** is the additional output that a company can produce by hiring one additional worker. The **marginal revenue product (MRP)** is the addition to total revenue caused by the last unit added to production. In a perfectly competitive industry MRP is simply MP measured or valued in dollar terms. For example, suppose the marginal (last) employee at a social work textbook manufacturer can produce five books an hour. The marginal revenue product is the MP (in physical terms) multiplied by the unit price of the output. If each social work textbook sells for $10, the MRP is $50 per hour ($5 \times \$10 = \$50$).

Equilibrium in the Labor Market

If the markets for labor and goods are in perfectly competitive equilibrium, workers are paid the value of their marginal product. Why are employers thought to behave this way? Employers do not want to pay workers the value of the company's marginal product; the interaction of supply and demand in the marketplace forces employers to pay workers their marginal revenue product.

The value of a worker's marginal product is a measure of how much the worker's labor is worth to a given employer. A rational employer will not pay workers more than they are worth but would love to pay them less. However, such a practice could not be sustained in a perfectly competitive labor market. Suppose workers in the textbook industry were paid $20 per hour (assume the MRP is still $50). Employers gain $30 more in revenue produced by the marginal worker than they pay in wages. They are making positive economic profits. As a result, more firms enter the industry, or firms already in the industry hire more workers, creating upward pressure on wages, downward pressure on the price of books, and downward pressure on the marginal revenue product of labor (because of the law of diminishing returns discussed in chapter 2). This pattern would continue until workers' wages equaled the value of their marginal product. Firms would bid up wages, or drive down the marginal product, until an equilibrium price and quantity were reached, with the wage equal to both the marginal revenue product of labor (the value that firms place on one more unit of labor) and the marginal disutility of labor (the value that individuals put on one more unit of labor).

Suppose instead that the wage is higher than the equilibrium wage. Many workers would want jobs, but few employers would be hiring. Workers would bid down wages until equilibrium was reached. Everyone who wants a job at the market wage has one, and every firm has as many employees as it is willing to hire at the market wage. At least, that is the way it would happen if the labor market worked perfectly, but the perfectly competitive labor market model is not without problems.

Criticism of the Competitive Theory of the Labor Market

Economists have used marginal productivity theory to explain the positive correlation between education and earnings.[5] That is, the more formal schooling people have, the higher their wages tend to be. One explanation for this finding is that formal schooling teaches skills that make workers more productive. The more productive they are, the greater their marginal product.[6] Social workers are very interested in the issue of poverty as it relates to working people. According to marginal produc-

tivity theory, one reason that the working poor exist is that their marginal product is low; increased education could increase their marginal
product. Government subsidies to help the working poor pay the costs of
obtaining more education is a policy that could help increase their
income. So would a policy that provided incentives for employers to pay
the costs of educating their workers.

Opponents of the redistribution of income and of minimum wage
laws often use marginal productivity theory to say essentially that the
only way to help the poor is to make them smarter. Proponents of the
redistribution of income often then throw up their hands and say that
economic theory is simply a justification for conservative economic policies. But, contrary to what some economists will lead you to believe, economic theory does not unequivocally support increased education as the
only solution to poverty. Suppose people with unskilled jobs learn new
skills and apply for jobs requiring more skills? What does the theory of
supply and demand say will happen to the wages of those occupations?
The supply of labor will shift out (see fig. 3.6), and the marginal product
and price (wage) of skilled labor will go down. The law of diminishing
returns means that putting more people to work in jobs requiring more
skills will drive down the return on those jobs, hurting workers already
in those jobs and helping the new entrants by less than expected. Is there
evidence that the law of diminishing returns applies to skilled labor? If
you lived in ancient Rome and you could read, write, and do basic arithmetic, you were easily a part of the upper-middle class. You could afford
a big house with lots of servants. Today, the minimum-wage worker
behind the cash register at Wal-Mart probably reads, writes, and does
basic arithmetic, yet she probably can barely pay her rent and cannot
afford any servants. Apparently, the marginal product of basic education
is lower now than it was two thousand years ago.

A similar argument could be made about welfare reform. Suppose
welfare reform succeeds in moving every so-called welfare mother into
the workforce. Proponents of welfare reform say this will make everyone
better off, but what does supply-and-demand theory say? More people
entering the labor market would cause a rightward shift in the labor supply curve (see fig. 3.6), driving down the marginal product of labor and
decreasing wages for lower-skilled jobs. Because many workers are
already living in poverty, such a policy will make the working poor even
poorer and will not move welfare recipients out of poverty. These conclusions follow from basic supply-and-demand economics, using the

assumption that wages equal the marginal revenue product of labor. These are not the one-sided conclusions that critics usually accuse mainstream economics of reaching.

Although the marginal productivity theory of wages is dominant in economics, the discipline is home to alternative views. This is not a labor economics textbook, so we will not delve too deeply into a discussion of such alternatives, but we will present one alternative view because of its relevance to the types of policy issues that interest social workers. One of the most articulate contemporary representatives of this view is Yanis Varoufakis, who draws heavily on the ideas of the nineteenth-century economist Karl Marx.[7] According to Varoufakis, the key mistake in the marginal productivity theory of wage determination is that it leaves out the role played by relative bargaining power in the determination of workers' wages. Potential employers and employees come together to consider entering into exchanges. Like all contracts, labor contracts contain the rights and obligations of the contracting parties. One of the most important terms is how much a worker will be paid.

Suppose Jean is the employee and Liz is the employer. How much Jean will be paid partly depends on how she could earn money if she chooses not to work for Liz. Jean's wage also depends on how easy it would be for Liz to find someone else to work for her if Jean decides not to. Suppose Liz offers Jean a wage of $5.15 an hour. Jean regards this wage as unfair but faces a problem: if she rejects the job, she is not eligible for any type of government assistance. Assume also that her society has no private charities and that Jean has no accumulated wealth to fall back on. All she owns is her ability to work. Imagine that most people in this society are in a position similar to Jean's. Given this situation, Jean would be faced with the following choice: work for an unjust wage and increase the probability that she will eat regularly or not work for this wage and perhaps starve. Because most people in the society are in Jean's situation, Liz is not under much pressure to pay Jean a higher wage. If Jean decides not to work for Liz, Liz can simply hire the next person on the brink of starvation and pay this person the $5.15 per hour wage.

Now assume that Jean and Liz are bargaining about Jean's wage, but this time the government gives every citizen $10,000 a year, enough to meet basic needs, whether citizens choose to work or not. Jean would now be under less pressure to work for Liz for an unjust wage, and Liz would be under more pressure to pay Jean a wage higher than $5.15 an hour.

According to Varoufakis, these scenarios illustrate the following points. Marginal revenue products do not determine workers' wages. Wages are determined by the relative bargaining power of employers and employees, which in turn is determined by the distribution of wealth, as well as by the particular social welfare and other institutions that exist. This means that social workers interested in increasing wages do not have to rely solely on policies that increase people's education levels. Relatively high unemployment benefits, welfare benefits, workers' compensation benefits, and the like can also increase wages by decreasing the pressure on people to work in low-wage jobs.[8]

A mainstream economist could respond that none of these observations conflicts with the supply-and-demand model. Labor supply would be higher in the first scenario than in the second. In other words, by increasing nonlabor income, the existence of social welfare and private charities would cause the labor supply curve to shift to the left (see fig. 3.7), resulting in a lower equilibrium quantity and higher equilibrium wage. Supply-and-demand theory says that an equilibrium wage will exist but does not say that the equilibrium wage will be higher than the poverty-level wage. Price in a perfectly competitive labor market equates the marginal revenue product of labor with the marginal disutility of labor. What is the marginal disutility of the labor of someone who faces a social (or physical) obligation to work? A person who is obliged to work would have a very low disutility of labor; that is, she would not have to be compensated much for the loss of leisure that results from working. Thus supply-and-demand theory provides at least one reason to believe that the equilibrium wage would be quite low.

Labor Market Discrimination

The National Association of Social Workers' (NASW) code of ethics states that "social workers should act to prevent and eliminate . . . discrimination against any person . . . on the basis of race, ethnicity, national origin, color, sex, sexual orientation, age, marital status, political belief, religion, or mental or physical disability."[9] Economists are also interested in discrimination, mainly as it relates to labor markets.

Mainstream economic theory has two major perspectives on labor market discrimination. One is associated with the widely acclaimed economist Gary S. Becker of the University of Chicago.[10] According to

Becker, some employers have a taste for discrimination. This means that some do not like certain people simply because they are members of particular racial or ethnic groups. For instance, some employers dislike African Americans, Japanese, or Puerto Ricans. Although Becker does not do so, his analysis could easily be applied to other groups, such as gays and lesbians, mentally ill people, or Christian fundamentalists.

Employers who have a taste for discrimination will not hire people from certain groups or will hire them only at a lower wage. If Jim dislikes Robert because Robert is openly gay, Jim will not hire Robert unless he is willing to accept a wage lower than the one Jim pays his heterosexual employees. In neoclassical terms Jim behaves as if Robert's gayness is an additional cost of employing him. Given the clause from the NASW code of ethics, social workers are typically interested in the formation of policies that attack practices like this. (According to a popular interpretation of Becker's analysis, if the labor market is perfectly competitive, such policies may be unnecessary because employers with tastes for discrimination will not last long in a perfectly competitive labor market.[11])

Suppose a small number of white employers with a taste for discrimination against blacks refuse to hire African Americans. The effect of this is a limitation on the pool of people who will be able to work for these employers (only nonblacks will be in this pool). In other words, by refusing to hire blacks, these employers drive up the demand for white workers, generating upward pressure on their wages. Meanwhile, blacks will compete with other workers for jobs with those employers that have no taste for discrimination, exerting downward pressure on the wages these employers have to pay. Thus employers who engage in fair hiring practices will have access to cheaper labor than the discriminatory employers will. This would give a competitive advantage to those with fair hiring practices and allow them to drive the discriminatory employers out of business. And with discriminatory employers driven out of business, social workers would be happy. An obvious response to this point of view is that because labor markets in the real world are not perfectly competitive, employers with a taste for discrimination may not be driven out of the market. Another response is that other theories of discrimination may be more realistic.

Some radical economists have argued that discrimination can be used in a divide-and-conquer strategy. Workers are more effective at gaining decent wages and working conditions if they are able, when necessary, to engage in collective action, such as strikes. Workers are in a better position to engage in collective action if no divisive issues separate them. Employers can create such divisions by discriminating against a chosen group.[12]

Another theory of labor market discrimination has to do with asymmetric information. When employers consider hiring someone, they have no way of knowing how productive a prospective employee will be; workers are much more informed about how productive they are than are employers. This information asymmetry requires employers to develop ways to estimate the productivity of potential employees. One way is to use what sociologists call ascriptive characteristics such as race and sex. The chosen characteristics may or may not be based on employers' past experiences with such workers.

For example, suppose an employer has heard that green-eyed employees are less productive than brown-eyed employees and decides not to hire any, not because of personal dislike of green-eyed people but because of lack of information. She simply uses green eyes as a basis for predicting how productive individuals will be. Economists use the term **statistical discrimination** to describe discrimination based on workers' observable personal attributes because of lack of information about productivity. The Harvard sociologist William Julius Wilson has found that blacks in the Chicago metropolitan area suffer a great deal from this kind of discrimination. (Wilson found that both white and black employers statistically discriminated against blacks, especially young black males.)[13]

To the extent that labor market discrimination is due to tastes, the way to curtail it is by changing people's tastes. It is not clear, however, what social policies would be appropriate for changing people's feelings about certain groups. There's truth in the adage that you cannot legislate morality. We can, however, enact legislation that authorizes those who feel they have been discriminated against to sue. This, of course, is the case in the United States.

Social workers tend to oppose discrimination because they believe it is unjust. It denies people human dignity, amounts to disrespect for people's cultural traditions, and is inconsistent with celebration of a multicultural society. Discrimination is also inefficient. Employers who have a taste for discrimination and those who discriminate to divide and conquer do not care whether those discriminated against are as productive as others. Employers who statistically discriminate are concerned with this question, but their use of ascribed characteristics as signs of productivity assumes the answer. Such employers may believe that black workers are less productive than whites when this is not really the case. Mistakes about productivity could cause employers to hire whites who are less productive than blacks. Discrimination based on any of these motives is inefficient and causes the level of goods and services produced by our economy to be less than it would be without discrimination. A social worker sophisticated enough to make the case that discrimination costs us in the form of less consumption would probably be taken more seriously in policy debates than one who grounds his arguments solely on celebrating multiculturalism or other objectives not necessarily well appreciated among the electorate.

Unemployment

Unemployment occurs when someone is willing and able to work and is looking for a job at the market wage but cannot find a position. Unemployment is an important topic in economics, but it is primarily in the realm of macroeconomics. This book focuses on microeconomics, so our treatment of unemployment will be very brief. Readers who are interested in learning more about economic theories of unemployment should consult a macroeconomics textbook.

The first and most important thing to understand about unemployment is that the economic definition of unemployment is different from the colloquial definition that you are probably familiar with. Most people who are not economists use the word *unemployed* as a synonym for *not employed*. A child, a student, a retiree, a full-time parent, and a person who is taking some time off before looking for a new job are all "not employed," but they are not "unemployed" in the economic sense. To be unemployed one must be willing, able, and looking for work at the market, or going, wage but unable to find it. People who are not working but are not willing to work at the going wage for whatever reason are "out of the labor force." A person who would work at a higher wage, who may even be looking for work, but who is not willing to work at the going wage is also considered to be out of the labor force.[14] The reason for the distinction between the unemployed and those out of the labor force is that the two conditions have different causes and different remedies. That some people do not choose to work at the going wage is not necessarily an economic problem, but that people who want to work cannot find jobs is a serious economic problem. It might be a problem if people do not want to work for the wages that are offered, but the solution to that problem is very different from the solution to unemployment.

Unemployment is a surplus of labor. As chapter 3 showed, a surplus is not supposed to last for long in a perfectly competitive market; if the quantity supplied is greater than the quantity demanded, the pressure on prices (wages in this case) will cause them to fall until an equilibrium is reached. At the equilibrium point the quantity that sellers are willing to sell equals the amount that buyers are willing to buy. A permanent surplus can exist in the labor market, although it does not exist in other markets, for four reasons. First, the labor market is not perfectly competitive. This explanation raises the question of what other model should be used. But none of the other models discussed in this book (monopoly, monopsony, oligopoly, and monopolistic competition) implies the persistence of surpluses. Second, the labor market is basically perfectly competitive, but the macroeconomy works differently than a single market. This explanation is beyond the scope of this book, although we will touch on it during the discussion of cyclical employment.[15] Third, there are enough jobs for people; it just takes a while for workers to find those jobs. We explain this situation during the discussion of frictional unemployment. Finally, the labor market is basically perfectly competitive, but wages either do not adjust or adjust very slowly to downward changes in demand because of minimum wage laws, unions, and the unwillingness of all workers to accept wage cuts.

Economists have identified three types of unemployment: frictional unemployment, structural unemployment, and demand-deficient (or cyclical) unemployment.[16] **Frictional unemployment** occurs when the number of job vacancies is equal to or greater than the number of people looking for work at the going wage, but some people remain unemployed because those seeking jobs have not been matched with those seeking workers. An individual is frictionally unemployed if there is a job out there for her, but it takes a while for her to find that job. Most economists agree that an economy with only frictional unemployment is at full employment. Economists disagree about how low unemployment has to go to be considered full employment. Some economists believe that an unemployment rate of 4 percent or even higher could be considered full employment; others would put the rate much lower.

An individual is **structurally unemployed** if the demand for her particular skills is insufficient to provide her with a job. That is, when the quantity supplied of a certain type of labor is greater than the quantity demanded. Plenty of jobs may exist for people with different skills, but not enough jobs are available for people with her skills. Structural unemployment results from wages that fail to adjust downward, the high cost of occupational and geographical mobility, and the high cost of retraining. It is possible to have a high amount of structural unemployment even in a fast-growing economy.

For example, suppose labor demand for electricians decreases, while demand for computer programmers increases. If the electricians market were perfectly competitive, the decrease in demand would lead to a lower equilibrium price and quantity. But suppose workers' refusal to accept pay cuts prevents the wage from falling to equilibrium. At this wage the quantity of labor that employers would be willing to buy would be less than the quantity that electricians would be willing to sell. In other words, structural unemployment would exist. If the unemployed electricians could become computer programmers at no cost, they could enter the computer programmers market. But they cannot do this so easily, and the structural unemployment in the electricians market could persist for a long time. Structural unemployment could lead to underemployment rather than unemployment if workers who are structurally unemployed from skilled jobs take jobs with lower skill requirements.

Cyclical unemployment, also called demand-deficient unemployment, is caused by a decline in aggregate demand in output markets. In this case the aggregate quantity of labor demanded is less than the aggregate quantity of labor supplied. In plain English the total number of job vacancies is smaller than the total number of unemployed. Aggregate demand is the total amount that domestic residents, businesses, government, and foreigners spend on domestically produced goods at each price level.[17] The aggregate quantity of labor demanded is the amount demanded by *all* firms in the economy, and the aggregate quantity of labor supplied is the amount supplied by *all* workers. If the demand for goods falls, the demand for labor will fall too, creating unemployment.

Unemployment has consequences that are important to social workers. The unemployed have a hard time obtaining the goods they need and often suffer from low self-esteem. They are more likely to get involved in domestic disputes, some of which may lead to separation or divorce. Unemployment also has a cost that may be of less concern to social workers but is of great concern to economists: Unemployment is inefficient, because society has to forgo the goods that would have been produced had the unemployed been working. Workers who want to work but cannot find a job are a resource that is being wasted. The efficiency loss from unemployment is the value of the goods that workers could have produced had they been working, plus the psychological costs that are of concern to social workers. Economists tend to focus on the cost of the lost output because it is easier to quantify, but they are aware that all costs associated with unemployment are part of the efficiency loss.

Unemployment is typically measured by the unemployment rate, which is the ratio of the number of unemployed to the number in the labor force. The labor force is made up of those who are working and those who are unemployed. For example, if a labor force of 100 million has 5 million unemployed people, the unemployment rate would be 5 percent (5 million ÷ 100 million = 5 percent).

The government keeps statistics on unemployment, but these statistics are far from perfect, and whether they underestimate or overestimate the unemployment rate is controversial. One reason that the government may underestimate unemployment is that it does not count discouraged workers as part of the labor force.[18] **Discouraged workers** are people who want a job but have given up looking for one and so are counted as out of the labor force. Suppose in addition to the 5 million people who are unemployed, another million are discouraged workers. If the government counted such people as part of the labor force and considered them unemployed, the labor force would increase to 101 million and the number of unemployed would increase to 6 million, making the unemployment rate just under 6 percent (6 million ÷ 101 million = 5.95 percent).

Another reason why statistics may underestimate unemployment is that the government counts underemployed workers as employed. An individual is underemployed if if he is unable to find a job that uses his productive capacity to its full extent. A person can be underemployed in two ways. Both part-time workers who would rather be working full time and people with high skills who cannot find a job in the high-skilled labor market and are forced to accept a job requiring lesser skills are underemployed. Some analysts believe the underemployed should be counted as unemployed.[19] Current statistics simply count the underemployed as employed, generating an underestimate of the actual unemployment rate. Suppose another million people are underemployed. If these people were counted as unemployed instead of as employed, the unemployed would number 7 million and the unemployment rate would be just under 7 percent (7 million ÷ 101 million = 6.93 percent).

On the other hand, official statistics may overestimate unemployment. Unemployment statistics are calculated on the basis of data obtained from interviews of or questionnaires filled out by a representative sample of the U.S. noninstitutionalized civilian population. All those who are not working outside the home, are currently available for work, and who have looked for work within the four weeks previous to being interviewed or filling out the questionnaire are considered unemployed.[20] Those collecting the data do not check on whether a person actually looked for a job within the previous four weeks or if the person is qualified for the job(s) he looked for. If 2 million of the people counted as unemployed did not really look for work within the previous four weeks (or are not really currently available for work), the unemployment rate would go back down to 5 percent (5 million ÷ 100 million = 5 percent).

Whether the unemployment statistics overestimate or underestimate unemployment depends on which of these effects is larger. But unemployment statistics do not count these effects because some are hard to measure; other reasons are related to politics. How can a surveyor know whether a person is truly underemployed or not? Before the Reagan administration, the unemployment rate included people who had been out of work for a long time but were still actively seeking employment. But the high unemployment rates were unacceptable, so the government simply recalculated how they were determined. Thus the best way to look at the unemployment statistics is as an index; although the unemployment rate is an imperfect measure of unemployment, it is safe to say that a low unemployment rate is better than a high one.

Another issue not captured in the overall unemployment rate is the variance by race, gender, age, and other factors. Blacks are more likely to be unemployed than whites. Men are slightly more likely to be unemployed than women are. People in low-income inner-city neighborhoods in Oakland, California, are more likely to be unemployed than people in the nearby wealthy suburbs of San Jose. Teenagers are more likely to be unemployed than adults. Black teens have the highest unemployment rate of all.[21] For example, the Bureau of Labor Statistics reported that the unemployment rate was 4 percent in January 2000. That makes it sound like everyone could find a job pretty easily, but at the same time the bureau reported that the unemployment rate was 3.4 percent for whites, 5.6 percent for Hispanics, and 8.2 percent for blacks. Therefore, the overall unemployment rate does not really give a good picture of how difficult it is for some groups to find a job.

Policies to Address Unemployment

Unemployment insurance provides a temporary income to unemployed people who were employed for a specific period in jobs covered by the program. It is financed by state and federal taxes on employers. This program is not intended to directly affect the demand for or supply of labor. It is intended, instead, to provide recipients with an income to tide them over until they find work. But just because unemployment insurance is not intended to affect labor demand or supply does not mean it does not have such an affect. The recipient is able to hold out longer for the job of her choice than she would be able to without unemployment insurance. This is another example of the income effect. Petra does not have to take the first job offered her if she is able to eat and pay rent without working.[22] Whether this is a good thing depends on your point of view. Those who believe able-bodied people have an obligation to work for their subsistence, regardless of wages and other work conditions, believe that this work disincentive is unfortunate.[23] Those who believe workers ought to have an alternative to working for low wages, perhaps under dangerous conditions, believe that the work disincentive is a good thing.[24] U.S. unemployment insurance attempts to strike a balance between these two positions. It is available only for a limited period of time and only for people who claim to be actively looking for work and who meet other requirements.

Demand-management policy addresses demand-deficient unemployment. The two kinds of demand management policy are called fiscal and monetary policy. **Fiscal policy** is the tax and spending policies of government. Imposition of a sales tax and increased spending on public works are examples of fiscal policies. When demand is too low, the government may increase spending or decrease taxes (increasing the size of the deficit or decreasing the size of the surplus) to try to get the demand for labor up. When demand is too high (which is believed to cause inflation[25]), the government may cut spending or raise taxes (increasing the size of the surplus or decreasing the size of the deficit) to decrease aggregate demand. An income tax cut and an increase in government spending would increase aggregate demand. Businesses would attempt to meet this increase in aggregate demand by producing more goods. Thus aggregate demand for labor would increase, decreasing unemployment.[26]

Monetary policy is the government's use of its influence on the money supply and interest rates. In the United States the Federal Reserve (the Fed), a component of the federal government, conducts monetary policy. The Fed essentially plays the role for the nation's banks that these banks play for us. Just as we borrow money from banks, banks borrow money from the Fed. Just as we pay interest on the money that we borrow, banks pay interest on the money that they borrow from the Fed. If aggregate demand is too high, the Fed can raise interest rates. If aggregate demand is too low, the Fed can use monetary policy to decrease unemployment by lowering the interest rate that it charges banks. Interest is simply the amount that a borrower must pay to use someone else's money. If banks are able to pay a lower interest rate to borrow from the Fed, they are likely to lower the interest rate that they charge the rest of us. This means that consumers are more likely to borrow to purchase cars or homes, and businesses are more likely to borrow to finance investment in new plants or equipment. Thus businesses will hire more workers to meet the increased demand for goods, decreasing unemployment. How effective fiscal and monetary policies are is highly controversial among economists.[27] Recently, the U.S. government has tended to rely more on monetary than fiscal policy, and it has tended to be more concerned with inflation than unemployment, but the question of whether the government should tinker with either is still controversial.

Providing information is one way to address frictional unemployment. A government agency could help employers and the unemployed find each other by serving as a clearinghouse. Unemployment insurance is also helpful for the frictionally unemployed. Government-provided education and training could address structural unemployment. If electricians lose their jobs because of structural unemployment in the construction industry, yet demand for computer programmers has increased, government could subsidize the training of electricians who want to become computer programmers.

Some economists believe that the minimum wage causes unemployment. Chapter 3 showed that a price maximum that is lower than the equilibrium price could cause a shortage. A price minimum that is higher than the equilibrium price can cause a surplus. If the price is not legally allowed to fall to the equilibrium level in a perfectly competitive market, the quantity supplied will exceed the quantity demanded, and a permanent surplus will exist. Proponents of this view point out that a price control exists in the labor market (in the form of the minimum wage) and a surplus exists. But this idea is quite controversial and the evidence is inconclusive; that is, no one has proved whether the minimum wage does or does not cause unemployment. Those who believe that the minimum wage causes unemployment have often called for its elimination or reduction. But this solution, even if correct, has one severe side effect. Reducing the minimum wage could reduce unemployment only by lowering wages so much that workers would be less willing to work and firms would be more willing to hire workers. Minimum wage workers already make poverty-level incomes. A decrease in the minimum wage would increase poverty among the working poor and give the unemployed jobs that pay poverty wages. This is hardly an appealing prospect for workers.

Because of their concern about the social problems that result from unemployment and other labor market problems, social workers have taken an interest in the development of policies that combat joblessness and low wages. Lowering the minimum wage is not an appealing solution for the problem of unemployment, because it will create more poverty-level jobs unless some other program exists to keep wages up. But stimulating demand may not be appealing because it may cause inflation. What else can be done? A few economists and sociologists believe that the best unemployment policy would be to treat the symptoms if we cannot cure the disease. They would advocate establishing a minimum income guarantee that ensures that people's incomes will not fall below the poverty line, even if they cannot find jobs.

Chapter Nine

The Economics of Poverty

In August 1996 President Bill Clinton signed into law a welfare reform plan that ended sixty years of social welfare policy. Since the passage of the Social Security Act of 1935, impoverished single parents with young children had had a statutory right to government assistance. The 1996 reforms turned welfare over to the states, removed the guarantee of assistance, stressed work instead of income assistance, and placed on recipients of welfare a lifetime eligibility limit of five years. Under this new system needy single parents with young children can simply be turned away if they appeal to the government for help during hard times. Although welfare is only one of many poverty policies, the debate that led to Clinton's signing of this legislation, as well as the ongoing discussion about how best to implement it, highlights the issue of how best to attack poverty.

Poverty, of course, has been a perennial concern to social workers. Many, often contradictory, theories describe the causes of poverty and have been used to support competing policies to address poverty. A good understanding of the theories behind poverty policy is essential to participation in the debate about what to do about poverty.

The Debate About the Definition of Poverty

According to the National Research Council, the two different conceptions of poverty are absolute and relative poverty.[1] According to the

absolute definition of poverty, poverty is the lack of income necessary to meet basic needs; according to the **relative definition of poverty,** poverty is the possession of an income that is less than some specific portion of median income.

The noted sociologist Lee Rainwater has argued that a relative definition is preferable to an absolute one because poverty is really about the inability of people to fully participate in their society. The best indicator of whether a person can participate is how his or her income compares to that of the typical member of society.[2] Thus poverty could be defined as earning less than one-half of the median income. One problem with this definition is that it seems to combine issues of poverty and inequality. For example, in a society in which the median income was $1 billion, a person with an income of $499 million would be considered poor. *Poor* may not be the best word to describe such a person.

The U.S. Census Bureau uses an absolute definition to calculate poverty statistics. The **poverty line,** or the **poverty threshold,** is the amount of income needed for a person or family to purchase the amount of goods necessary for survival. A family with an income below the poverty line is considered poor. The Census Bureau calculates the number of people living in poverty (below the poverty line) and the poverty rate (the percentage of people living in poverty) for the United States. The bureau determines the poverty line by calculating the amount of money that families of various sizes need to purchase a minimum level of food and then multiplying by three. The government uses this method because, when it was developed in the 1960s, economists believed that most families spent about one-third of their income on food.[3] The U.S. Census Bureau collects data on family income, and any family with an income that falls below the poverty line for families of its size is considered poor. According to the bureau, the poverty line for a family of four in 1999 was about $17,000. In 1999 the number of poor people was about 31 million and the poverty rate was 11.8 percent.[4]

The Census Bureau's methodology has been criticized a great deal.[5] First, the family income that is compared to the poverty threshold does not include in-kind benefits such as Medicaid, food stamps, and public housing. If these benefits were considered as income, many people classified as poor would not be. Thus some have argued that leaving out in-kind benefits leads to an overestimation of poverty in the United States.

Second, the Census Bureau's definition of the poverty line does not take into account differences in the cost of living in different parts of the country. A poverty line income of $17,000 buys much more in Mississippi than it does in New York. Whether this problem causes an overestimation or an underestimation of poverty in the nation as a whole is not clear, but it certainly skews our perception of where poverty is most prevalent.

Third, the current definition of the poverty line fails to take into account differences in necessary expenditures such as health care. Suppose the Beauregard family has four members, one of whom has a congenital disorder that requires the family to pay $4,000 a year in out-of-pocket medical costs. The Beauregards' annual income is $18,000. Thus, after they pay their health-care costs, the Beauregards have $14,000 left for all other expenses. On the other hand, the Passer family also has four members, all of whom are healthy; they pay no out-of-pocket health-care expenses. The Passers' income is $16,000 a year. Given the Census Bureau's definition of poverty, and the current poverty line of $17,000, the Passers are poor and the Beauregards are not, even though the Beauregard family has less money to spend after paying its health-care expenses. Because many of the working poor with incomes near the poverty line have no health insurance, leaving out medical expenses probably leads the Census Bureau to underestimate poverty.

Fourth, multiplying the cost of food by three to determine the poverty line does not reflect changes in relative prices and consumption behavior since the 1960s. At that time most families did spend about one-third of their income on food, but today some researchers say that most families spend only about one-fifth or one-sixth of their income on food. If the Census Bureau multiplied food expenditures by five instead of three, the poverty line for a family of four would be more than $28,000 ($17,000 ÷ 3 × 5), and many more people would be defined as poor.[6]

Fifth, this definition of poverty does not consider how much an individual works or the wage rate available to that person. For example, suppose Debra works one full-time job at the minimum wage and earns an income that is below the poverty line. Jerry has the same skills and opportunities as Debra, but he works two full-time jobs at minimum wage, bringing his income above the poverty line. According to the Census Bureau, Debra is poor but Jerry is not. But in an economic sense Jerry is just as poor as Debra is; Jerry feels his poverty in less leisure time, and Debra feels her poverty in less consumption of other goods.

Although the U.S. Census Bureau uses one specific definition of poverty, the academic debate about how best to define poverty is far from settled. The best thing about the current poverty line, however, is that it exists. It may be arbitrary, but it provides a reference point from which to assess changes in poverty. The poverty rate may not tell us the exact percentage of the population that is having serious financial difficulty, but an increase in the poverty rate says that things have gotten a little worse for people with low incomes and a decrease says that things have gotten a little better. Therefore, this chapter uses the Census Bureau's conception of poverty despite its faults.

Trends in Poverty and Social Policy in the United States

The modern history of social welfare policy in the United States begins with the Great Depression of the 1930s. Following the stock market crash of 1929 and the bank failures of the early 1930s, the nation saw a massive downturn in economic activity and a massive increase in unemployment. National income declined by one-third during a four-year period, and the economy reached a point at which nearly 1 in 4 workers was out of work. The government at the time offered few social services for the poor and found itself unable to deal with such a crisis. President Franklin Roosevelt took office in 1933 and responded to the Great Depression with massive new social programs, including Social Security, Aid to Dependent Children (which later became Aid to Families with Dependent Children, or AFDC), and many others. The first federal minimum wage law was introduced, as were laws protecting labor rights and unionization.

The Great Depression disappeared virtually overnight when the United States entered World War II in 1941. The war created a demand for labor that greatly increased wages and employment. The GI Bill provided for school and college tuition for all veterans after the war. Because such a large percentage of Americans had fought in the war, these programs had an enormous effect on economic inequality in the United States. By the 1950s the United States was far more prosperous and far more economically equal than at any time in its past. The government did not then keep official poverty statistics, so inequality is the best measure of material deprivation. But poverty was still with us. In 1959, the first year in which official statistics were kept, the poverty rate was 22.4 percent.[7]

In the 1960s President Lyndon Johnson declared his War on Poverty.

Congress expanded New Deal programs such as Social Security and AFDC, increased the minimum wage, and introduced new programs such as Medicaid. By 1973 the poverty rate had been cut in half, to 11.1 percent. Enthusiasm for the War on Poverty gradually faded, and many of Johnson's programs were cut back, especially under President Ronald Reagan in the 1980s. Poverty began to gradually increase, topping 15 percent at times in the 1980s and early 1990s. The economic boom of the 1990s helped bring poverty back down to 12.7 percent by 1998.[8] However arbitrary the poverty line may be, the steady decrease in poverty from the 1950s to the early 1970s and the increase from the early 1970s until the mid-1990s reveals something important about poverty in the United States. Despite continued economic growth since 1973, the poorest Americans have shared little of the economic boom, although the poor had shared in the gains from growth between the end of World War II and 1973. The difference is a matter of considerable debate within the economics profession; some economists blame the changing nature of the global economy, whereas others blame the reduction in social welfare programs since the 1970s.

Theories About the Causes of Poverty

The academic literature tends to focus on six probable causes of poverty: inadequate demand for labor, unequal power in the marketplace, inadequate human capital, inability to work, lack of work ethic, and labor market discrimination. These causes are not mutually exclusive; more than one or all may contribute to poverty.

INADEQUATE DEMAND FOR LABOR (THE LOW DEMAND THEORY). According to this view, the demand for labor may not be high enough to absorb all those who are willing and able to work at an adequate wage. Low demand for labor could be a temporary or chronic problem. Most often, people speak of low demand as causing unemployment, but it could instead or as well cause employed workers to earn wages that put them below the poverty line. Obviously, either unemployment or low wages can lead to increased poverty. Unemployed workers themselves are likely to be poor, but low demand also puts downward pressure on the wages of employed workers (see chapter 3). If the labor market is not regulated, nothing about its functioning ensures that the prevailing wage will be sufficient to keep workers above the poverty level.[9]

UNEQUAL POWER IN THE MARKETPLACE. Another theory of poverty, which is mostly associated with Marxian economics but is advocated by other schools of thought as well, is that workers do not enter into exchanges with employers as equals and thus are forced to accept low wages, regardless of their productivity.[10] If unequal power in the marketplace, rather than low demand, is the explanation for poverty, wages are not equal to workers' marginal revenue products. But the two theories have more in common than one might think. In both the more workers there are relative to the number of job openings, the lower wages will be; in both the more workers need to get a job to survive, the lower wages will be.

LOW HUMAN CAPITAL. As defined in chapter 1, human capital is the skills, knowledge, and abilities that make people more productive on the job. If the labor market is perfectly competitive, people with more human capital will receive higher earnings than those with less human capital. According to some economists, people with low human capital end up either unemployed or employed in poverty-wage jobs because their productivity makes it unprofitable for firms to pay them above-poverty wages or, in some cases, to hire them at all.[11] Some evidence exists that those with less formal education are more likely to be poor than those with more formal education.[12] This finding could be regarded as evidence that human capital has at least some effect on poverty. A broad definition of human capital can also include physical abilities and disabilities, but because the solutions to such problems are very different, it might be best to treat them separately.

INABILITY TO WORK. People may be unable to work for many reasons. Physical reasons include being too old, too young, or physically disabled. Other reasons include family responsibilities such as caring for a young child or a sick relative. People like to think that a clear divide exists between those who can and cannot work, but in fact all the reasons for being unable to work have arbitrary, culturally determined cutoffs. The difference between a person who cannot work and a person who should not have to work is great, yet attitudes often confuse the two. Some people cannot work past the age of sixty-five, yet others are capable of working past one hundred. U.S. citizens have made a statutory decision that no one older than 65 should have to work, but the cutoff point could as easily be 64, 66, 59, or 71. Blind people cannot become forklift operators, but they can become lawyers. Yet U.S. citizens have given blind people the option of receiving disability for life if they so choose. Certainly, people with severe cognitive limitations or mental illnesses cannot work, but those with intelligence levels slightly higher than that deemed indicative of a cognitive disability are expected to work. Ten-year-olds can work, but most people in the United States believe they should not have to. Legally, children younger than sixteen are not allowed to work in most nonfarm industries, but people are allowed to buy products made by children in other countries. As discussed later in this chapter, in the 1930s the belief that single mothers should not work (outside the home) was widespread; today prevailing opinion seems to have completely reversed, and all single mothers on welfare must seek employment. Certainly, many people cannot work, and many others should not have to, but drawing the line between those who can and those who cannot is an extremely difficult normative issue.

LACK OF WORK ETHIC. This view of poverty has to do with cultural commitments. Some able-bodied people may identify with groups that adhere to cultures that devalue work. The political analyst Lawrence Mead is perhaps the most articulate proponent of this view. He bluntly contends that an insufficient work ethic causes most poverty. He believes that most of those who work full time year-round are not poor and that most of those who are poor do not work full time all year. According to Mead, the main difference between most of the able-bodied poor and most of the able-bodied nonpoor is that the nonpoor believe that they have an unconditional obligation to work, while the poor believe that they should work only if wages and work conditions are ideal. In other words, the nonpoor value work sufficiently, whereas the poor do not value it enough. Because the poor do not value work enough, they end up not doing much of it, or doing a poor job of it, and fall to the bottom of the income spectrum.

LABOR MARKET DISCRIMINATION. According to this view, employers systematically exclude certain groups from better jobs because the employers tend to believe that people in these groups are less capable or the employers simply do not like the group. Estimating the extent to which this causes poverty is difficult because the result closely resembles the results of other proposed causes of poverty. If employers are unwilling to hire people from a certain group, the demand for labor in the geographic areas where this group is concentrated will be low. Members of groups that are excluded from the better-paying jobs might be more likely to develop the idea that work is of little value, less likely to make investments in enhancing their human capital, and less likely to develop a strong work ethic. These individuals might end up poor, but their poverty would appear to be caused by inadequate demand for labor, lack of human capital, or lack of a work ethic, when ultimately the real culprit is labor market discrimination. Whether discrimination is or is not a cause of an individual's poverty is a positive (not a normative) issue (positive economics deals with what is or will be, and normative economics deals with what should be). The relationship of poverty and discrimination is so difficult to determine that views of discrimination often become a matter of opinion.

The Problem with Poverty Policy:
The Efficiency-Equity Trade-off

The **efficiency-equity trade-off** is a commonly discussed problem relevant to any policy to redistribute income; the term refers to the notion that policies intended to redistribute income in order to promote equity also curtail efficiency. Recall from chapter 3 that an unregulated economy with perfect competition in every market would produce an efficient outcome. Any deviation from that outcome would reduce the total amount of goods available to society as a whole. Some economists have explained this hypothesis using the analogy of a leaky bucket. Robinson Crusoe has more water. Friday has less, but the only way to transfer water from one to the other is a leaky bucket. Thus the only way to redistribute water from one to the other necessarily reduces the total available to both. Why must this happen? First, remember that it is inevitable *only* in a society with perfect competition in every market and then only when the product of human effort is being redistributed. In a perfectly competitive economy all people are rewarded by what they, and their property, produce. Giving money to the less productive means taking it away from the more productive, which in turn gives both less incentive to be productive. Plus some overhead cost is involved in transferring resources; labor, which could otherwise be used to produce goods, is needed to run the organization that transfers goods from one person to another.

Is an efficiency-equity trade-off unavoidable? No—more than one hundred years ago John Stuart Mill demonstrated that, even within a competitive economy, the final distribution of goods depends on the initial distribution of goods. Redistributing the final distribution of goods causes an efficiency-equity trade-off, but redistributing the initial distribution of goods does not. There is not one efficient outcome but a different efficient outcome for every initial distribution of property rights.[13] More recently, economists have downplayed the importance of Mill's observation by saying that the initial distribution of property rights has only a small effect on the actual distribution, because only a very small portion of wealth is inherited. Whether they are right is a difficult empirical question. Another criticism of the efficiency-equity trade-off is that the economy is not made up of perfectly competitive industries. Thus not all income rewards some person's marginal product, and opportunities for taxes and transfers may exist that have little or no detrimental effect. Those who believe discrimination is a primary cause of poverty tend to believe that the efficiency-equity trade-off does not exist, because discrimination is itself inefficient. Eliminating racism and any other "ism" at its source would therefore simultaneously increase both efficiency and equity.

Too often people base their opinion of the efficiency-equity trade-off on their belief about whether income should be redistributed. People who oppose redistribution usually believe that the efficiency-equity trade-off is significant; people who favor redistribution tend to dismiss any claim that such a trade-off exists. Both attitudes are unwise. Whether such a trade-off exists and how big it is are positive questions. An efficiency-equity trade-off may exist, but the trade-off may be worthwhile to relieve poverty. To permit concern for the poor to obviate any concern for an efficiency-equity trade-off is to ignore two questions that are crucial to determining an effective way to reduce poverty. A close look at the current welfare system reveals fairly plainly that many of its strategies are in fact leaky buckets, but this is not sufficient to conclude that it should be scrapped. Many questions remain. Which antipoverty policies have a smaller efficiency-equity trade-off? How can we reduce the efficiency-equity trade-off for any given policy? And if more equity does imply less efficiency, how much inefficiency are we willing to accept to increase equity?

Policies to Address Poverty

Strategies to address poverty fall into two broad categories: government and private charity. We focus on government policies to address poverty, but some policymakers advocate turning all questions of poverty over to private charities. However, for private charity even to maintain the level of poverty relief that the government provides would require an enormous leap in charitable activity. Living without the government programs would most likely mean permanently living with much higher levels of poverty.

Government policies to address poverty also fall into two broad categories: categorical and universal. The categorical approach requires a different policy for each cause of poverty. The universal approach has one policy for all causes of poverty. The categorical approach allows the government to choose policies that are appropriate to the individual's situation. The government may decide that some poor are ineligible for help because they are not seen as truly needy. Because the United States has tended to emphasize the categorical approach more than the universal one, and because our intention in this book is to apply economic tools to the analysis of policy issues in this country, most of the policies discussed here are elements of a categorical approach.

Policymakers and academics have identified six approaches to ameliorating poverty, including greater economic growth, workfare, the minimum wage, wage subsidies, public employment, and guaranteed income. The first four are aspects of the current system, and last two are proposed reforms.

Aspects of the Current System

ECONOMIC GROWTH. One of the most popular ways to attack poverty is to increase economic growth, which would mean more goods would be available for everyone. This policy is most helpful if low demand for labor is the primary cause of poverty. The hope is that these goods become available to more and more people in terms of a greater demand for labor and more or better jobs for everyone, including the poor. Two theories, almost polar opposites, explain how the government can increase economic growth and the demand for labor.

Keynesian theory supposes that the economy tends to get caught in a trap of insufficient demand for goods and labor.[14] Firms would be willing to hire more workers if they thought they could sell more goods, and consumers would be willing to buy more goods if only more jobs were available. Thus the economy can become stuck (some say temporarily, some say permanently) with high unemployment. The hope is that the government can increase the demand for goods by decreasing taxes, by increasing spending (increasing the size of the budget deficit), or by lowering interest rates (see chapter 8). Then more demand for goods would increase demand for labor to the point that employment and wages increase, thus reducing poverty.

Neoclassical economists believe that overstimulating the economy is worse than understimulating it.[15] They believe that unemployment tends to settle at a natural rate and that any attempt by the government to use demand stimulus to reduce unemployment below its natural rate will ultimately cause inflation and will not reduce unemployment in the long run.[16] Some neoclassical economists believe that Keynesian policies to stimulate demand are appropriate if—and only if—unemployment is higher than the natural rate; other neoclassical economists believe that the government should never stimulate demand. Most neoclassical economists believe that the best way to stimulate employment in the long run is for the government to get out of the way and let businesses invest and expand. Thus these economists tend to recommend lower taxes and fewer regulations. Critics labeled this policy "trickle-down economics" in the 1980s, when Reagan suggested that lower taxes on businesses and wealthy individuals would eventually help the poor as well.

In short, Keynesian economists believe that *more* government action and neoclassical economists believe that *less* government action will stimulate growth and lead to high employment. For this reason Keynesian economics is often considered liberal and neoclassical economics is considered conservative, but these characterizations are too simplistic. If a natural rate of unemployment exists, demand stimulus cannot reduce unemployment, but that does not mean that the government should do nothing to help the unemployed; it simply means that if the goal of policy is to help the disadvantaged, the government must find a more effective strategy. Whether demand management can reduce unemployment continues to be one of the most controversial issues in economics.[17]

Although maximizing economic growth is important in its own right, any strategy to maximize it is an indirect solution to poverty. Indeed, these issues would not belong in a chapter about poverty policy if people did not argue so often that the best way to attack poverty is to increase growth. This is sometimes used as an argument against more direct policies to address poverty. However, economic theory does not lead unambiguously to the conclusion that growth reduces unemployment. More economic activity could mean greater demand for workers in general, but it could as easily mean greater demand for workers with certain skills, while workers with other skills or fewer skills fall further behind. Or greater economic activity could be accompanied by automation and the "de-skilling" of jobs that leads to more jobs at lower wages.

The historical record hardly supports the contention that growth is the best cure for poverty. The 1940s and 1960s were periods of high growth and decreasing poverty, but these were also periods in which the government was active in addressing poverty directly. The 1920s and 1980s also were periods of high growth but, many analysts agree, increasing poverty and inequality. The twentieth century as a whole saw an enormous amount of growth but did not see poverty disappear. Therefore, we seem to have little reason to believe that economic growth alone will cure poverty in the foreseeable future.

Even if we assume that fiscal and monetary policy can significantly reduce unemployment, these policies address directly only one of the proposed causes of poverty—inadequate demand for labor. They may also, in a sense, address discrimination in the labor market if the labor market is so tight that employers with tastes for discrimination against certain types of workers are forced to hire them or to forgo the revenue they could earn from exploiting their labor. More demand for labor could give workers a little more market power and more ability to bargain for higher wages, but it cannot change the basic power relationships of the employment market. A better labor market might give those with little work ethic more of an incentive to adopt one, and might encourage people with low human capital to increase their skills, but this relationship is obviously quite indirect and is not likely to eliminate these problems. A better labor market is of no direct help to those who cannot work, but they may have relatives who work, or the population might be more willing to support generous programs for those who cannot work in times when labor demand is tight.

Current government policy seems to follow the neoclassical view of growth. The government seldom uses fiscal policy specifically to affect demand. The Fed uses monetary policy to put the brakes on the economy as often as it uses monetary policy to stimulate it. The prevailing wisdom at the Fed seems to be that demand stimulus alone is insufficient to bring the unemployment rate below 4 percent or the poverty rate below 12 percent.

WORKFARE. The 1996 welfare reform act changed Aid to Families with Dependent Children (AFDC) to Temporary Assistance for Needy Families (TANF). It was also characterized as a switch from "welfare" to "workfare." The idea of workfare is to have recipients work for their benefits and to encourage them to move into the private labor market as quickly as possible. TANF recipients, even those with very young children, are required to work or prepare for work in return for their benefits. Work includes working in parks, social service agencies, schools, and other mostly public and nonprofit institutions. Preparation for work includes enrollment in secondary school and classroom-based job training programs. TANF recipients who do not take part in these activities risk the loss of a portion of their benefits.[18]

Public discussion of workfare tends to focus on the extent to which it succeeds at moving recipients from welfare to work, with less attention to its effect on poverty. If this policy succeeds in reducing welfare rolls by increasing the supply of labor, it could decrease wages for the working poor; if so, it could hardly be called a success at reducing poverty.[19] To make matters worse, some evidence suggests that low-wage employment has detrimental social consequences, including crime.[20] If so, the increased likelihood of becoming a crime victim might be the cost that society pays for using workfare to move more people from welfare to work.

Clearly, a large part of the rationale for workfare is the belief that a lack of work ethic is a major cause of poverty, at least among single parents. The change from AFDC to TANF represents a great change in attitudes toward single mothers that occurred gradually in recent decades. When AFDC was introduced in the 1930s as part of a broad categorical strategy to alleviate the Depression, single mothers were widely believed to be in the category of people who could not, or should not, work. By the time TANF was introduced, the prevailing attitudes had changed greatly. Many proponents of welfare reform seemed to believe that all single mothers could and should work (that is, participate in the labor market) and that the availability of AFDC had caused many of them to lose the work ethic. Even if welfare recipients do lack a work ethic, whether workfare will cause them to develop one is questionable. Forcing people who do not place a high value on work into the lowest-status, lowest-paying jobs in the economy may not make them value work.

Those who ascribe to the human capital theory of poverty might view workfare approvingly, but to make TANF truly a program that enhances human capital would require a major revision of it. Workfare is ostensibly designed to increase the skills, work experience, and education of welfare recipients. However, many of the jobs offered to workfare participants, such as picking up garbage in parks, may not provide people with opportunities to enhance their human capital at all.

The workfare approach does nothing to address poverty that results from an inadequate demand for labor. In fact, it might even increase poverty if inadequate demand is a problem. On the basis of simple supply-and-demand theory, all else being equal, if workfare succeeds in moving more people into the labor market, the result could be a decline in wages both for new entrants and for those already employed. An increase in supply leads to a higher equilibrium quantity (more employment) at a lower equilibrium price (lower wages). Because 10 percent of employed Americans are already earning poverty-level wages, a decrease in wages would increase poverty even if a rise in employment and a drop in the welfare rolls accompanied it.[21] If, on the other hand, low demand for labor results in unemployment instead of low wages, an increase in the labor supply will just increase the number of unemployed. A very serious contradiction exists between the welfare policy of TANF and the demand management policy of the Fed. TANF tries to get more people into the labor market, assuming there will be enough jobs, but the Fed tries to keep unemployment from getting too low lest it spark inflation.

Those who believe that an unequal distribution of power in the marketplace is a significant cause of poverty do not view workfare favorably. They claim that workfare is not empowering to workers in the low-wage labor market; if anything, it will make workers more dependent on employers and less able to bargain for higher wages. It may not do much to address poverty caused by labor market discrimination, either. Even if workfare increases the human capital of participants, as long as they are disproportionately members of a discriminated-against group, such as African Americans, the increase in human capital may not be enough to encourage private-sector employers to cease indulging their tastes for discriminating. In other words, workfare does nothing to stop employers from making hiring decisions on the basis of seemingly irrelevant criteria such as race.

THE MINIMUM WAGE. One strategy for reducing poverty, at least among workers, is to mandate a significant increase in the minimum wage. The minimum wage is $5.15 per hour, approximately $10,000 per year before taxes. However, it would have to be increased by more than 65 percent, to at least $8.50 per hour, to bring a family of four to the poverty line. The minimum wage can certainly increase the wages of many workers, but many economists believe that it also has serious side effects that can harm some workers.

As discussed in chapter 8, using supply-and-demand analysis, a minimum wage above the equilibrium wage will cause a labor surplus—a situation in which the quantity of workers supplied is permanently higher than the quantity of workers demanded. That is, it will cause unemployment. There is a large amount of debate, on both theoretical and empirical grounds, about whether the minimum wage actually does cause unemployment, and the empirical evidence is mixed.[22] If the minimum wage does cause unemployment, the question becomes whether the trade-off is worthwhile—does the number of workers helped by the higher wages justify the cost to those who become unemployed, and what can society do for those who are unemployed? Whether a minimum wage will cause the quantity of labor demanded to decrease or not, it is unlikely that it will increase the demand for labor; therefore, this solution alone will not help those who are unemployed and may even make it harder for them to find jobs.

If unequal power in the marketplace is the explanation for low wages, the minimum wage is more attractive. If workers are paid less than what they are worth because of their lack of bargaining power, a minimum wage can raise incomes without necessarily causing unemployment. A minimum wage obviously does little for those who are unable to work unless they have relatives supporting them who do work. If the cause of poverty is a lack of work ethic, a minimum wage could make work more attractive, but for it to have any real effect may require a much higher minimum wage. If low human capital is the problem, the minimum wage could give employers more incentive to train workers, but it cannot ensure that employers will want to hire all the additional workers, and it is not a solution for those who have a severe difficulty working.

Some economists believe that a minimum wage will actually make it easier for employers to discriminate by making the number of applicants for a given job larger and by not allowing applicants to compete by offering their skills for a lower wage, thus giving firms greater leeway to hire whomever they like. Other economists believe that discrimination happens by channeling certain workers into the lowest-paid jobs; if so, although a minimum wage cannot prevent discrimination, it can increase the wages of those who get stuck in the lowest-paid jobs.

WAGE SUBSIDIES. This policy essentially adds government money to a worker's paycheck. The United States has had a wage subsidy plan since 1975 called the Earned Income Tax Credit (EITC). The program was established to offset the adverse effects of payroll taxes on the working poor and to increase the incentive to work. The EITC is a refundable tax credit, which means that if the amount of the credit to which a family is entitled exceeds the amount it owes in taxes, the family receives a refund check from the government. If a family earns too little to owe federal income taxes but qualifies for the EITC, the family receives a check from the Internal Revenue Service. Up to a point, the amount of the credit *increases* as a person's income increases, and the credit is gradually phased out at higher income levels so that workers always have an incentive to earn more.[23]

The EITC does not enhance workers' skills, but because it does offer low-skilled workers more money, it could be helpful if inadequate human capital causes low wages. Obviously, the EITC does little or nothing for those who are unable to work, and it cannot help the unemployed because it does not increase the demand for labor, but it could be helpful if inadequate demand for labor causes low wages. Like the minimum wage, it may be able to lessen the monetary effect of discrimination or low market power, but it does not eliminate the causes of these problems. The EITC may make work more attractive to those with little work ethic, and unlike the minimum wage, it doesn't have the potential side effect of making employment more difficult to find. However, the EITC is rather small and lifts above the poverty line the incomes of only a small portion of its recipients (those with incomes already near the poverty line). That workers can still end up poor even if they receive the EITC suppresses the extent of what might be called its work ethic–enhancing aspects.[24] The small size of the EITC makes it a barrier to being much help whatever the cause of poverty.

OTHER ASPECTS OF THE CURRENT SYSTEM. The programs mentioned thus far are only a few of the many programs that have an effect on poverty. Social Security has been so effective at reducing poverty among the elderly that it is easy to forget that it is an antipoverty program and to think of it instead as a pension program. But before Social Security the incidence of poverty was much higher among the elderly than among younger people; now poverty is much lower among the elderly, and the decline in poverty among the elderly was one of the primary causes for the drop in overall poverty up to the 1970s. All levels of public education raise human capital and certainly have a great, if indirect, effect on reducing poverty. Antidiscrimination laws are designed in part to do the same. Unemployment insurance, though available only temporarily, undoubtedly helps many of those who are eligible to keep from falling into poverty while they are between jobs. In-kind programs such as food stamps, Medicare, Medicaid, and public housing, although they do not count as income and therefore do not affect the official poverty rate, certainly help many poor people to maintain a higher standard of living. But even with all these programs working together, the unemployment rate remains higher than 4 percent and the poverty rate remains higher than 12 percent.

Overall, the U.S. poverty strategy follows the categorical approach. Social Security helps those who cannot work because they are old, disability payments go to those who cannot work because they are physically disabled, unemployment insurance assists those who cannot find work, the minimum wage and EITC help those who find work at low wages, TANF is available to single parents (and others), and so on. Few programs are for the poor simply because they are poor, and many people living below the poverty line are simply not eligible for any kind of government assistance.

The rationale behind this categorical strategy is twofold. First is the normative belief that government should help only those who are willing to work or those who cannot work and all others should fend for themselves. Second is the positive belief that a categorical approach can reduce the efficiency-equity trade-off. If the government could "costlessly" separate those who can work from those who cannot and help only those who can work, these programs could alleviate poverty without harming anyone's work incentive. But as we have seen, it is not easy to separate those who can from those who cannot work, and much of the expense of current government programs is not the actual money that is redistributed but the overhead expense of determining who is eligible under the rules. Many economists believe that this expense overwhelms any savings that might be gained by separating out those who can and cannot work. In fact, the difficulty of separating those who can and cannot work creates work disincentives. For example, seniors who want to work face the loss of some or all of their Social Security if they do; people on unemployment insurance lose the entire amount if they take a job, so they may be afraid to take a job until their benefits run out. Nearly all categorical programs create such disincentives, so it is widely believed that the categorical strategy has a rather high efficiency-equity trade-off.

Two Reform Proposals

THE GUARANTEED JOB. The idea of the government's simply hiring all the unemployed has been proposed in different forms for many years. The Works Progress Administration, which hired many of the unemployed, was introduced temporarily during the Great Depression.[25] The economist Hyman Minsky proposed a comprehensive version in 1986, and this idea has been kept alive by a small group of economists ever since.[26] A comprehensive version of the guaranteed jobs approach would go a long way toward simplifying the current system and making it more universal. It could replace all income assistance programs for those able to work (including TANF, unemployment insurance, the minimum wage, EITC, etc.). The government would ensure that anyone willing and able to work would be able to get a job in the public sector (which is why the approach is often called the public jobs approach, or the employer of last resort).

A government jobs program could eliminate the problems caused by inadequate demand for labor. It could directly eliminate unemployment.[27] If the public sector jobs paid wages higher than the poverty level, it could eliminate poverty among the working poor as well, because few if any workers would work at below-poverty wages for private-sector firms if public jobs were available at higher wages.

Public jobs may or may not increase an individual's human capital. These jobs could be designed with on-the-job training to enhance workers' skills, but public jobs could simply employ the limited human capital that people have. A potential conflict exists within a guaranteed jobs program between the desire to put workers to work and to train them. Although training may be better for the recipients in the long run, a focus on training would take the program away from its mission of providing a guaranteed job. If the program enhances human capital, it could lead people to higher lifetime earnings. If it does not, it may at least provide the low skilled with secure jobs at above-poverty wages.

To the extent that the absence of the work ethic causes poverty, the guaranteed jobs approach might face some problems. If able-bodied people were entitled to income support only if they agreed to work for it, they might develop a greater work ethic. However, it might be difficult to both guarantee people a job and give workers at that job an incentive to work hard. An important issue that a guaranteed jobs program would have to resolve is whether workers could be fired for poor performance. If so, the program would arguably not be truly a guaranteed jobs program, as workers who are fired would become unemployed. But if workers were not held accountable for their performance, would they really be working? Perhaps there are ways workers could be held accountable for their job performance without including the option of firing them for bad performance. This is an important—but not necessarily insurmountable—issue that designers of a public jobs program would have to address.

A guaranteed job obviously cannot help those who cannot work, although it is a very comprehensive policy for those who can. It would certainly go a long way toward reducing poverty; combined with a strong program for those who cannot work, it could be part of a categorical approach that could eliminate poverty. It would also go a long way toward empowering workers who would always know they had the option of participating in public-sector jobs rather than the private-sector market, and if public-sector workers were allowed to unionize, every employer in the country would have to pay wages comparable to unionized public-sector workers.'

Perhaps the biggest drawback to a guaranteed income program is its price tag. The cost includes not only the wages of all the public sector workers but the wages of supervisors and support staff and the cost of work space and work materials. The overhead costs could add up to more than the wage cost. However, the value of the goods produced by these workers must be subtracted from the costs. Supporters of the guaranteed jobs approach believe that it either would have a low efficiency-equity trade-off or that it would actually be efficiency enhancing because it would put people to work who are not working. Critics contend, however, that if the overhead costs are high and the productivity of these jobs is low, the guaranteed job could have a substantial efficiency-equity trade-off.

THE GUARANTEED INCOME. *Guaranteed income* is a catchall term for a number of similar plans (including basic income, the negative income tax, the social dividend, and many others), all of which unconditionally guarantee a certain minimum income to all citizens and all of which ensure that the more private income that people earn, the better off they will be. This chapter does not discuss the technical differences between various guaranteed income plans but focuses on what they have in common.

In a guaranteed income scheme two numbers are important: the minimum income level and the tax rate, or the benefit reduction rate.[28] The minimum income level is the amount of money that someone without a private income would receive. The benefit reduction rate is the rate at which the minimum income would be reduced or earnings would be taxed as private earnings increase.

For example, suppose a system was constructed with a guaranteed annual income of $10,000 for a family of three and a 50 percent benefit reduction rate (meaning that for every dollar a family earns, it loses $0.50 of its supplement or pays a $0.50 tax on its earned income). A family with no earnings receives the $10,000 minimum. If this family earns $2,000, its benefits are reduced by $1,000 (50 percent of $2,000), amounting to a net income of $11,000 ($10,000 + $2,000 − $1,000 = $11,000). If this family's earnings increase to $10,000, its after-tax income is $15,000 ($10,000 + $10,000 − $5,000 = $15,000). If its earnings increase to $20,000 (the break-even point), the amount of taxes the family pays just equals the income supplement it receives ($10,000 + $20,000 − $10,000 = $20,000). Only those families that make more than

$20,000 in private income would be net taxpayers. Note that this family is always better off monetarily by increasing its earned income rather than relying solely on the income guarantee.

The guaranteed income does not directly address the various causes of poverty discussed in this chapter, but it does effectively address the symptom. If the minimum income guarantee were set high enough and benefits were dispensed regularly, the policy could abolish poverty, regardless of its causes. Even though a guaranteed income might not affect the demand for labor, it might increase wages. If people were able to get their basic needs met without having to work, both supply-and-demand theory and theories of market power predict that workers would be able to command higher wages in the labor market.

Critics of a guaranteed income include those who believe a poor work ethic causes poverty. They believe that more people would choose to stay home and receive the minimum income instead of going out to work. In an effort to determine the extent to which a guaranteed income might decrease the labor supply, a number of experiments using different versions of the guaranteed income were conducted in the United States in the 1970s. The analyses of the data from these experiments are quite technical, so we won't discuss them in detail. In a nutshell, most analysts believe that those who were eligible for a minimum income decreased their work effort. The studies also found that women decreased their work effort more than men did.[29] On the basis of these findings some might argue that a guaranteed income would be a dangerous way to address poverty because it might create too drastic a reduction in the labor supply. Before jumping to this conclusion, however, recall that employers might respond to a guaranteed income by increasing wages; this would at least partially offset the work disincentive effects of a guaranteed income. Also, a guaranteed income has a higher work incentive than some categorical plans (such as disability and unemployment insurance) in which workers lose their entire benefit if they make any private income at all.

Although a guaranteed income might not directly affect the level of human capital, it might do so indirectly. If people were able to survive without having to work, they could allocate more of their time to going to school or volunteering to work in environments where they might learn productive skills. Thus in the long term a guaranteed income might generate an increase in productivity (how much workers produce each hour they work), which might improve societal well-being. Even if it does not increase human capital, the guaranteed income ensures that those with low human capital are not destitute.

The Normative Economics of Poverty

Most of this chapter has dealt with positive economic issues, but the most important issues in a topic like poverty are normative. Remember that positive economics deals with what is or will be, and normative economics deals with what should be. Ultimately, opinions about poverty policy depend primarily on individuals' normative beliefs, that is, on their conception of social justice. The normative question of what the government's responsibility toward the poor is divides opinion into at least four groups—those who believe the government has no responsibility, those who believe the government has a responsibility to the "truly needy" but not to others, those who believe the government has a responsibility to provide some equality of opportunity but no equality of outcome, and those who believe the government has a responsibility to provide a minimum standard of living to all citizens. Most often, people's positive and normative beliefs are consistent. People who believe the government should not redistribute income also tend to believe that redistribution is quite harmful to economic growth, whereas those who believe that the government should redistribute income tend to believe that doing so will not have harmful side effects.

People who believe in the redistribution of income often too easily dismiss criticism that certain methods of redistribution will not work. People who believe in less redistribution tend to exaggerate the difficulties with doing so. Your opinion of what should be must not cloud your understanding of what is and vice versa. A good understanding of both the normative and positive sides of any issue has no substitute. We hope that the understanding of the positive issues you have gained from this chapter will help you understand what means may be effective in achieving normative goals.

of the prices that other providers are charging for these services. Suppose Henry is feeling a little queasy and goes to see a physician. He explains that he is having stomach pains, and the doctor prescribes a remedy. Because Henry is not trained in medicine, he is in no position to judge the quality of the physician's prescription. He could wait to see if his pains go away, but the disappearance of his pain may or may not be related to the quality of the doctor's treatment. Also, even if it were possible to determine the quality of the doctor's treatment after the fact, at the time of the exchange the doctor is more informed about the quality of her intervention than Henry is.

The inability of health-care consumers to assess the quality of health services means that incompetent or unethical physicians may be able to deceive them. For supply and demand to determine the optimal quantity, demand must represent the price that consumers are willing to pay for a given amount of benefit that they receive from the goods provided. But when receiving health care, consumers rely on producers to tell them how beneficial their services will be. Once consumers get sick, the situation becomes even more complicated because they have little opportunity to shop around for the best deal and could not easily compare the quality of two different service providers if they did shop around. If individual consumers cannot make an informed optimal choice about their own purchases, the market cannot determine the optimal quantity for society as a whole. In the worst case a medical procedure may actually harm a consumer. The possibility of an exchange that is not mutually beneficial may justify government intervention in health-care markets.

Clients who receive services from social workers are in a similar position. If Julia feels depressed and decides to see a social worker, she is unlikely to be able to judge the quality of this counseling, unless she has training in psychology and counseling techniques. Therefore, she is not in a position to judge the quality of the psychosocial assessment, psychoanalytic intervention, or cognitive behavioral intervention that she receives. Some legislators have proposed that the government license social workers to help ensure quality. If consumers themselves cannot determine the competence of a social worker, perhaps a government examining board can use the results to decrease the likelihood that consumers will suffer at the hands of incompetent practitioners. However, licensing is not a perfect protection from incompetent practitioners. The states require that doctors be licensed, but they cannot protect consumers from unethical practitioners. Licensing can even make unethical

behavior easier if the licensing procedure is controlled by unethical practitioners who are more interested in reducing competition than ensuring quality (see the section in chapter 7 on rent seeking).

Many analysts who have studied the health-care industry argue that
managed care has made the problem of imperfect information more significant than it once was. Managed care is an attempt by insurance companies to contain health-care costs by controlling both the payment for
medical procedures and the decision of what kinds of procedures are
allowed. It is a mechanism designed to hold down medical care costs,
partly by rationing care. Before managed care became widespread in the
1990s, most medical insurance was handled under the **fee-for-service**
system, in which physicians were paid according to the number of services they provided. The worry at that time was that physicians had no
incentive to contain costs and would prescribe costly, unnecessary procedures, driving up the cost of medical care without improving patient
well-being. Managed care is attractive because it provides incentives to
contain costs, both by eliminating unnecessary procedures and by
emphasizing less expensive preventative care, thus benefiting patients as
well as insurance companies. The danger of managed care is that it also
gives health-care providers an incentive to deny necessary medical procedures because the insurance company makes more money if it provides payment for fewer procedures.

One strategy used by many managed care insurance plans is **capitation,** which pays physicians a set fee based not on how many services
they provide but on how many patients they care for. For example, Dr.
Peter Price has an agreement with the Stony Brook Managed Care Company (Stony Brook). The agreement stipulates that Price is responsible
for providing care to fifty of Stony Brook's policyholders. Under the fee-
for-service system Stony Brook would pay Price a fee for each service he
provides to any of the policyholders he is responsible for treating. The
fee-for-service system would give Price no incentive to contain costs. He
makes more money if he provides more procedures, so he has an incentive to prescribe the most expensive procedures as often as possible, even
if he is not entirely sure they are necessary.

Under capitation Stony Brook pays Price a set fee for the fifty people
in his caseload, regardless of how many services he provides to these
patients. If he is able to keep his costs below the amount he receives from
Stony Brook, he makes a profit. If his costs rise above this amount, he
incurs a loss. The lower he can keep his costs, the more money he will

make. Thus he always has a monetary incentive to reduce the number of procedures that he performs. One way that Price can keep his costs low is to encourage his patients to get exercise, eat well, and avoid risky behavior like smoking; if he keeps them healthy, he will not have to provide much care to them. Also, Price no longer has any incentive to prescribe expensive unnecessary procedures. But what worries many critics of managed care is that Price has another way to keep his costs low: by advising patients against undergoing procedures that might help them but are expensive. The problem of imperfect information means that patients rely on the doctor to tell them whether they really need care, and they cannot judge for themselves whether they are getting the care they need. Capitation puts the monetary interests of doctors into direct conflict with the interests of patients. Doctors may be ethical enough to ignore these financial incentives, but no one can be sure that all doctors will be at all times, especially if they are operating near the break-even point.

Consumers are allowed to sue physicians and social workers for malpractice. We can think of such laws as government interventions to address the problem of imperfect information. If practitioners can be held liable and punished for harming consumers, they have an incentive to engage in more careful and ethical practice. However, some laws protect managed care companies from being sued for malpractice. The logic behind this legislation (aside from the immense political power of managed care companies) is that managed care companies do not make decisions about what health care an individual needs or should have; the company only makes decisions about what health care it will pay for. If a doctor mistakenly tells you that you do not need care, you may not get it simply because you are unaware of the need. If a managed care company tells you it will not pay for care that your physician says you need, nothing—other than the expense—stops you from getting it anyway.

Critics of managed care have argued, however, that physicians and social workers make decisions that result in patient suffering because of pressure by managed care officials. Managed care companies attempt to get providers to ration care not only by paying them capitated fees but also by informing providers that they will be compensated for only a specified amount of care.[1] For example, Alison Bell is a social worker who is seeing a clinically depressed client. A managed care firm that has a contract with Bell insures the client. The contract stipulates that Bell will be reimbursed for the care she provides to the client for as many as eight sessions, but if Bell sees the client for more than eight sessions, the managed care firm will not compensate her. Suppose Bell has seen the client eight times and believes he is still depressed and in need of treatment. She may not be able to afford to provide further treatment free of charge, and the client may not be able to afford to pay for it out of pocket. Thus she terminates the client, and shortly thereafter he attempts to kill himself. As the law stands, Bell but not the managed care company would be liable.

Congress recently considered a measure that would have allowed patients to sue managed care companies for the denial of care. One argument against the bill was that it would cause managed care companies to increase premiums, thereby increasing health insurance costs for consumers. The reasoning is that if managed care firms regard the possibility of being sued for malpractice as an increase in costs, the supply of insurance would decrease and the equilibrium premium would increase. The extent to which this view may be right depends on the nature of the health insurance market. If the market is competitive, insurance companies have no market power and must pass all their costs on to consumers, either in the form of higher prices (if demand is inelastic) or in the form of fewer services (if demand is elastic). If the market is monopolistic, increased costs may increase price or reduce service but will also cut into industry profits. A policy-oriented social worker would have to obtain empirical data about the price elasticity of demand for health insurance, the market structure of the industry, and the profitability of firms before and after the regulations went into place in order to assess the extent to which critics are right about the consequences of the bill that Congress is considering. An increase in costs certainly could mean that some consumers would no longer be able to afford insurance or that some providers would go out of business, but even if this argument is correct, it does not mean that we can do nothing. It means that a law allowing suits will have difficult side effects, which might imply that some other strategy could better achieve the goal. It does not mean that the goal is not worth pursuing.

Imperfect information is not the only efficiency-based justification for government intervention in health-care markets. The discussion of externalities in chapter 5 addressed another such justification. Recall that government subsidized the cost of treating an indigent homeless man suffering from tuberculosis because the man's treatment generates a positive externality by reducing the possibility that others will become infected.

Equity-Based Government Interventions in Health Care

Economists make a distinction between efficiency issues and equity issues. Generally speaking, economists are uncomfortable considering equity issues because they feel their training in economics provides no special competence in this area. Many economists think such questions should be left to philosophers and theologians, but some tacitly address equity issues. If economists were to stick entirely to positive questions (questions of what is), they would be unable to give any opinion on any issue with equity considerations. They could say what the efficiency costs of a policy option might be, but they would be unable to make any judgment about whether efficiency gains are worth the cost. Some economists make pronouncements on equity issues based on efficiency criteria alone. Economists who do this are far from leaving considerations of equity to philosophers; they are tacitly saying that equity considerations have no value. This behavior should not be accepted. A good student of policy must understand both efficiency and equity issues and must not ignore either. Because this is a book about applied economic theory, it has kept considerations of equity to a minimum, but equity considerations play a crucial role in some economic issues and cannot be ignored. Health care is one of them.

About 42 million U.S. residents had no health insurance in 1998.[2] Those without health insurance are at higher risk of disease and death and are less likely to receive medical services than those with health insurance. Some believe that society has a responsibility to provide health-care services to all individuals, even if they cannot afford to pay for them. Others believe that individuals are responsible for making enough money to pay for their own health care. The discipline of economics (and this book) cannot resolve the philosophical debate between these two points of view, but it can help assess the effectiveness of plans aimed at making health care available to more people.

Whether U.S. residents should have a right to health care or not, the government has implemented programs that appear to be based on the belief that such a right exists. Medicaid is a means-tested program intended to provide health care to the indigent. Medicare is intended to provide health care to the elderly; it is not a means-tested program. The United States also has public clinics and hospitals that are legally obligated to provide care, regardless of a patient's ability to pay. The belief that everyone has a right to health care also appears to be the basis for one of the most far-reaching proposals to reform the health-care system yet imagined: universal health care.

Economists would say that the nation does not have the resources to provide all the health care that everyone wants. Social workers are likely to respond by saying that the United States could provide all the health care its residents need. This, of course, raises the difficult philosophical question of what health-care needs are. Do we need only care that will keep us alive? Does that include extremely expensive procedures that will extend the life of a very ill person in extreme pain by only a few days? Do we need only that care that will maintain us in a state of well-being? If so, how do we know when we have reached a state of well-being? Do we need only that care that will make us feel physically and emotionally well? If so, what if an elderly person would feel well only if he looked younger and could look younger only if he received plastic surgery? Would he *need* plastic surgery?

An economist is likely to answer these questions by saying that notions of what people need are so subjective that health-care needs are essentially no different than health-care wants. Need cannot be positively (objectively) defined, but we as a society can determine on a normative basis what medical procedures ought to be considered needs, and we could meet those needs by saving money in other areas. If, under a universal health-care system, some limit would have to be placed on what people were entitled to, some grave ethical issues would arise. For example, Genie is a ninety-five-year-old woman who is hospitalized and has just slipped into a coma. Her physicians feel that she is unlikely to come out of the coma but could live for some time if she were put on life support. If this were done, her care would cost about $2,000 a day. Should Genie be entitled to life support? Paul is a five-year-old boy who is suffering from the measles. Treatment that would lead to a full recovery would cost $100. Should Paul be entitled to measles treatment? Pedro is a two-week-old infant who was born prematurely. During birth his heart stopped, and physicians have said that his brain was deprived of oxygen for about three minutes. Pedro is now in a coma on life support, and no one knows whether he will ever regain consciousness. Nor does anyone know whether his brain will function normally even if he does. Pedro's care costs $4,000 a day. Should Pedro be entitled to this care?

No doubt, readers will have different opinions about whether a universal health-care plan should pay for the care of each of these people.

What someone thinks may depend on what happens to the money not spent on treatment. If not treating Genie means $2,000 a day in higher profits for an insurance company, many people (who are not stockholders of the insurance company) might be more likely to say she should be treated than they would if not treating her meant that twenty Pauls would be saved from the measles every day. But even then people will have substantial differences about what they believe to be necessary care. Differences in people's opinions about what should constitute the standard benefits package will be largely based on differences in values. If we grant the assumption of scarcity, we would somehow have to transcend such value differences in order to arrive at some agreement about a standard benefits package. In a country as ideologically diverse as the United States, this would not be an easy task, and the package would always be controversial. But let us assume that a benefits package has been decided upon and turn next to the question of how to provide it.

This section discusses the potential economic consequences of three approaches to universal health care, each of which would provide all U.S. residents with access to a standard set of benefits. The discussion is limited because the main contribution that economics can make is by examining the ramifications of the three approaches.

First, the play-or-pay plan, which received a great deal of attention during President George H. Bush's administration, would require employers either to provide health insurance to their employees or to pay a special tax that would be earmarked to finance health care for the uninsured. One consequence of the play-or-pay plan could be that it would lead to an increase in the price of goods or to a decrease in wages in industries that do not already provide health insurance for their employees. If employers were required to provide care to their employees or pay a health-care tax, their costs would increase. Unless firms reduced wages or some other cost, supply of whatever they produce would decrease, leading to an increase in price and a decreased quantity in output markets. The extent to which employers would be able to raise prices would depend on market structure and the price elasticity of demand in affected markets. Whether universal health care is worth the risk of higher prices is not a question that economics can answer; it is one each citizen must answer: Is universal health care worth the trade-off? But the first step toward addressing this question is another question: What is the trade-off?

Second, managed competition, which was proposed by the Clinton administration, would allow those not already in Medicaid or Medicare to purchase health insurance through their employers or through new government agencies organized by the states. Employers who provide health insurance and their employees would be required to pay a specific proportion of their premiums. Self-employed and unemployed people would have to pay out of pocket for their insurance but would be eligible for government subsidies. All employers would have to pay a payroll tax to finance the subsidies. The Clinton administration anticipated that most self-employed and unemployed persons would purchase insurance from the new government agencies. Architects of the proposal envisioned that employers and government agencies would then bargain with groups of providers and insurers to obtain the best deals for their employees and group members. Because the Clinton approach would require employers to pay part of their employees' health insurance premiums and an increased payroll tax, it too could lead to price increases for goods. This plan would probably spread the increased costs around more industries than the play-or-pay plan.

Third, the single-payer plan is based closely on existing health-care systems in Canada and Europe but has received less attention in the United States. Under this plan the federal government would essentially become a large health insurance company. Some combination of federal income taxes, payroll taxes, or other taxes would finance the plan, in effect serving as insurance premiums. The federal government would allocate these revenues to state health agencies that would use the money for the budgets of hospitals, clinics, and other health facilities and to compensate individual health-care providers. The levels of these budgets and compensation would result from negotiations between representatives of providers and health facilities and the state agencies. Under the single-payer plan individuals would not have to pay out of pocket for their health care.

Depending on the types of taxes that financed the policy, the single-payer approach could also lead to price increases, wage decreases, or more unemployment. However, some analysts believe that the single-payer plan could yield cost savings and decrease prices. This argument is based on the idea that eliminating profit-making insurance companies from the health-care market would allow the government to more ethically contain costs. Opponents of the single-payer system believe that government mismanagement would increase costs more than this strategy would decrease costs. The only way to know for sure is to try the system. But evidence for cost savings from a single-payer plan is that countries such as Canada and Britain, both of which have a single-payer system, tend to have citizens who are as healthy as those in the United States but have considerably lower health-care costs. In addition to saving on advertising and administrative costs, eliminating insurance company profits, and paying doctors less, these plans save money by limiting the use of expensive medical procedures. The money saved by rationing more expensive procedures stays in the system to provide health care that is more cost effective. These savings, however, do not deny the basic economic notion of scarcity. It comes from making an important decision about what to trade off. Countries with single-payer systems tend to be much better at providing treatment to Pauls, but the United States tends to be better at providing treatment to Pedros and Genies. If you need a prescription drug to keep your high blood pressure under control, you are better off in Canada; if you need a helicopter to take you from the bottom of a cliff to the shock-trauma unit of a high-tech hospital, you are better off in the United States.

Another economic aspect of an equity intervention like universal health care has to do with moral hazard. Recall from chapter 5 that moral hazard occurs when insurance provides people with incentives to engage in behaviors that increase the likelihood of the events insured against. For example, before Jean got health insurance, she was a careful driver, did not smoke, and had a healthy diet. After she became insured, she started speeding, smoking, and eating salty corn chips for dinner. She knows that all these activities increase the likelihood that she will suffer health problems but engages in them anyway because she realizes that someone else will be paying for her health care. The moral hazard problem regarding universal health care simply means that more "Jeans" would exist than do now.

Social workers are likely to be skeptical about the existence of moral hazard in health care. Surely, concern about the pecuniary cost of health problems is not the main reason that people engage in healthy behaviors. People maintain a healthy diet and drive carefully because being healthy feels better than being unhealthy. Headaches, broken bones, and cancer are painful and disfiguring conditions that people want to avoid. These concerns are more than enough to restrain the extent to which any decline in monetary health-care costs would lead to an increase in unhealthy practices.

Economists and social workers probably agree here more than they disagree. Economists would be the first to recognize that health care entails costs other than pecuniary ones. They would also recognize that these nonmonetary costs could be so high that monetary costs are insignificant by comparison. Where they probably part company with social workers is that economists focus on marginal factors. Even if the money cost of health care is only a small part of the cost of unhealthy behavior, a marginal decrease in money cost can cause a marginal increase in risky behavior. Of course, careful empirical research would be necessary to determine what kind of moral hazard the health-care market would encounter.

The Economics of Organ Transplantation

An issue that has received increasing public attention is organ transplantation.[3] Most discussions of transplants have dealt with the question of the equity of the mechanism used to allocate organs. The fairness question is obviously important, but here we will focus on efficiency, using the the Pareto-improvement criterion. The place to begin an economic consideration of organ transplantation is with the recognition that organs are, in the economic sense, scarce goods. That is, the number of organs available is smaller than the number of people who need them. Moreover, the extent of scarcity has been increasing. Between December 1987 and December 1991 the total number of patients on organ transplantation waiting lists increased by about 75 percent. The number of people who died while waiting for an organ doubled between the early 1980s and the early 1990s. About 33 percent of patients die while awaiting a matched donor.

Currently, the organ transplantation system in the United States is administered by the United Network for Organ Sharing (UNOS). UNOS keeps a list of all transplantation candidates. Its job is to distribute organs fairly, based on seriousness of need and time spent waiting for an organ. The organ transplantation system is voluntary and is motivated by altruism. That is, people are allowed to choose whether they want to donate their organs, and they do so out of concern for helping others. They are not allowed to obtain monetary compensation in return for their donations. A perennial problem is that the number of organs donated annually is not large enough to meet the need. Concerned parties are considering ways to get more people to donate, and several policies have been proposed.

One proposal is mandated choice. Under this proposal everyone who reaches a certain age would be required to decide whether to be an organ donor. This would occur when upon renewal of a driver's license, filing income taxes, or performing some other task mandated by government. This proposal would not necessarily result in an increase in the number of organs donated because people would still have the right to refuse to donate their organs.

Another proposal is presumed consent. Hospitals would be allowed to harvest organs unless the deceased had explicitly forbidden them to do so. In other words, silence on the donation question would be taken to mean yes. Depending on how many people would explicitly refuse to donate, this proposal could lead to a significant increase in the number of donated organs.

A third proposal is routine retrieval. Under this approach organs would be harvested from all deceased people, regardless of whether they had agreed to donate when alive. Exceptions would be made only for religious reasons, with objections made formally in advance. Of the three proposals discussed here, this would probably lead to the greatest increase in the number of organs available for transplantation. This increase, however, would come at the expense of what some might consider an unacceptable escalation of government intrusion into people's lives.

Another approach involves the creation of a market in human organs. We will discuss this option at length because it is the approach most relevant to economics. This proposal has three components. Living donors would be allowed to sell their nonessential organs while they are still alive; presumably, most organs sold by such people would be kidneys. Living donors would be allowed to sell the right to their organs once they are deceased. Families would be allowed to sell the organs of recently deceased relatives. The relevance of economic theory to this proposal ought to be clear. If people were able to obtain money in return for selling their organs, they would be more likely to provide them, and they would save more lives. Thus both sellers and recipients of organs would be made better off without anyone else being made worse off; that is, a Pareto improvement would occur.

Social workers and many others, including some economists, are likely to be troubled by this line of reasoning. The buying and selling of human organs strikes many people as morally wrong, whatever its effects on Pareto efficiency. Can we say that there is an externality because some people find the practice offensive? Under a very loose definition of externality, yes. However, if what you do has an externality just because some other people dislike your choice, the door is open to seeing nearly everything you do as an externality to someone: An externality is involved if some people disapprove of your church, your choice of reading material, what you eat for dinner, and whether you color your hair. You can engage in hardly any activity that someone else might not disapprove of. If many activities widely regarded as human rights are seen as externalities, they could be discouraged or banned. For this reason it may be better to think of an externality as something that *directly* affects a third party. For example, if your next-door neighbor cooks on his barbecue and his smoke goes onto your property or into the environment, that's an externality. But if you just don't like it that he eats barbecued food, that's not an externality. Those who oppose the sale of organs may have to look elsewhere for a justification. How can we draw the line between what *directly* affects someone and what doesn't?

One efficiency justification for a nonmarket approach is that relying on the market may not bring out the best organs. Blood banks have cut back on the practice of paying for blood donations because studies found that people who sell their blood are more likely to have a blood-borne disease than people who donate their blood. A similar situation could develop with organ donations, but no one would know for certain unless the practice was tried. The equity reasons to ban the sale of organs may be more convincing.

One equity problem is that if organs were bought and sold, the rich would be able to obtain them easily, the poorest people would sell them routinely, and the middle class would have great difficulty affording them if they needed them. Many people believe that the ability to pay is an ethically unacceptable criterion for determining who receives an organ transplant. Another equity consequence of authorizing a market in human organs is that it could cheapen human life. Some people believe that if body parts could be sold like refrigerators, we might come to value them no more than we value refrigerators. Needless to say, many would find this outcome deeply offensive. Economists are less likely to engage in such considerations because doing so requires a perspective on markets that they usually do not adopt. When economists focus on markets, they tend to be concerned with whether the markets lead to efficient outcomes, given the preferences of consumers.

Chapter Eleven

Economic Demography

How do people decide how many children they will have? Do welfare payments encourage poor women to have more children? Is the family declining—and what is a family, anyway? Why do people get married—or divorced? Why do people move? Do the states' levels of welfare payment play a role in the decision to move? Are economic development packages a good deal for the taxpayer? How can we save the Social Security program as the baby boomers begin to retire?

These may seem like strange questions for the science that studies buying and selling, but economists have found ways to apply rational choice theories and supply-and-demand models to topics that are far removed from the marketplace. Critics have accused economists of academic imperialism, saying that economics seems no longer to be a discipline that specializes in the study of the economy but a discipline that specializes in the use of rational choice theory in any conceivable context. Because economists are applying their methodology to problems once considered the realm of other disciplines, a good understanding of economic theory is more important for all other social scientists.

The Economics of Fertility

People choose to become parents for a number of reasons, such as to carry on the family name, to have someone to love, or to carry out their religious duty. Following the influential approach of Gary S. Becker, economists who study fertility tend not to pay much attention to these reasons, not because they think the reasons are unimportant but because they think they are not germane to the construction of a useful model of fertility decisions.[1] Economists let other social scientists worry about why people want things, whether a child or a car. Economists focus on how people respond to costs and constraints, given their wants. The economist asks what factors will influence people who want children to have more or fewer of them?

Demand is the relationship between the price of a good and the quantity demanded, all other factors being equal. Just as with any other good, the demand for children (how many children people decide to have) depends on the cost of children.[2] Let's face it: People do incur costs when they decide to have and raise children. Economists use the opportunity cost of children as the "price" of children in defining the demand for children. Thus the economic theory of fertility amounts largely to looking at the cost of children. If the cost of children declines, the quantity of children demanded will rise and vice versa.

The cost of having a child includes the price of all the things a parent will have to buy for that child in its lifetime, plus time the parent will have to spend with the child.[3] Although parents enjoy buying things for their children and spending time with them, these are still costs: One dollar spent buying something for a child is one less dollar that is available for buying anything else. One hour spent with the child is one less hour that is available to do anything else, including working. Therefore, the time and money that a parent devotes to a child represent the opportunity cost of a child.

Estimating the cost of everything a parent will buy for a child in the child's lifetime is easy, but how do economists measure the price of the allocation of time? Recall from chapter 1 that the opportunity cost of something is what must be forgone to obtain it. The opportunity cost of spending time with children can be measured by the parent's wage, whether that time would have been spent working or at leisure—if she is already choosing the optimal amount of leisure time, the marginal benefits of work time and leisure time are equal. Thus economists use forgone earnings to attach monetary values to the time spent having and rearing children.

Suppose Julia decides that if she has a child, she will have to drop out of the labor force for four years and for years after that will be able to work fewer hours than she otherwise would have.[4] She also will lose work experience and will have much less time available to spend at other leisure activities such as playing tennis. Thus the time cost of having a child is all the lost wages she could have earned in the time she would have spent working, plus the lifetime loss in earnings resulting from four years' loss of work experience, plus the value of her lost leisure time.

If the law of demand holds, the relationship between the quantity of children demanded and the cost of a child is negative: the higher the cost, the smaller the quantity demanded. Thus, if women's wages were to increase, fertility rates would decline. Economists have focused on the wages of women because they give birth and typically have been the primary caretakers. Some evidence supports the contention that the relationship between women's wages and fertility rates is negative.[5]

The model of fertility discussed thus far has been the basis for work on the relationship between out-of-wedlock fertility and welfare. A number of public officials and social commentators have argued that out-of-wedlock fertility is at the root of many of the social problems plaguing the United States. Some officials and commentators have also argued that welfare is a major cause of out-of-wedlock fertility. The rational choice approach can be applied to out-of-wedlock fertility, just as it can to fertility decisions in general. If an indigent unmarried woman has a child, she may be eligible for welfare. Also, if a single woman on welfare has another child, her subsidy often increases. These aspects of the welfare program in effect lower the cost of rearing children. Thus economists would predict a positive relationship between welfare and out-of-wedlock fertility. Welfare does not need to pay the *entire* cost of having a child to increase out-of-wedlock fertility, because people want to have children. If something someone wants becomes relatively less expensive, the person is more likely to demand it even if it is still not free. The problem here is that policies that are designed to make it easier for single parents to get by also encourage women to become single parents.

A number of studies suggest that although the relationship between welfare and out-or-wedlock fertility is positive, it is not very strong. In other words, other factors—such as years of schooling and socialization—appear to have a greater influence on fertility decisions among single women.[6] Thus policies that curtail welfare benefits for single parents or deny recipients increased benefits when they have more children apparently will do little to decrease out-of-wedlock fertility.[7] One provision of the 1996 federal welfare reform legislation allows states to deny increased benefits for welfare recipients who have another child. Although most members of Congress are not economists, they presumably based their decision in part on a model of fertility similar to this one.

Much of the literature read by social workers features a cultural argument that pertains to out-of-wedlock fertility. According to this view, unmarried women are more likely to have children than they were in the 1950s because social norms have changed. In the 1950s unmarried mothers were more likely to be socially ostracized than they are today. That is, they were more likely to be viewed as immoral, disowned by relatives, or shunned by the rest of their community. Although economists often leave such cultural considerations out of their models, including them is easy. Being punished for having a child out of wedlock is a cost. Thus a decrease in the likelihood of being punished can lead to an increase in the quantity of children demanded by unmarried women.

In using economics for understanding fertility decisions it is important to recognize the factors that contribute to the demand for children. Wages, welfare rules, and social norms all affect the cost of having children. Economic theory can give you an idea about whether these factors are likely to lead to an increase or a decrease in the demand for children, but theory alone cannot reveal how important each factor will turn out to be. Empirical studies may give some indication of the size of the effects. Understanding how policy decisions are likely to affect fertility requires an understanding of the theory and how well that theory has held up to empirical scrutiny.

The Economics of Marriage and Divorce

As most social workers are probably aware, there is a debate in the United States about "the decline of the family." Several trends are thought to be indicative of this decline, including the higher divorce rate and the number of people having children out of wedlock (despite the drop in the teen pregnancy rate). First, are these trends really indicative of a decline in the family? If *family* means two heterosexual parents who are married to each other and live together with their children, *decline* might be the correct term to use. But perhaps the definition should be broader, which might mean that the family should be thought of as changing instead of declining. From the point of view of economic theory, whether the family is declining or changing does not matter, because economists are interested in what accounts for different kinds of family forms, not how they are viewed morally or politically.

Marriage is a contract. Two parties make certain promises to each other, many of which have important financial implications for both. These promises are, of course, often made within the context of certain religious rituals and symbols. Such practices notwithstanding, some aspects of marriage are similar to other contracts, such as publishing agreements, mortgages, or business partnerships.

As you might expect, economists typically examine marriage using the rational choice model. People get married if the benefits exceed the costs. What are some of the benefits of marriage? Because married couples often pool their incomes and other resources, one benefit might be a larger budget. Other gains might be more sociological. A couple may receive approval from their families and their community. Some government tax policies favor married people. People also get married because they enjoy spending time together, but this need not enter the decision-making process because people can spend as much time together as they want without getting married. However, one of the more significant benefits of marriage is a legal commitment (a contract) to stay together and to support each other.

What are some of the costs of marriage? Two costs are the ceremony and the marriage license. Although some tax policies favor marriage, others make marriage more costly.[8] Marriage can also lead to increased costs of decision making. If Jill wants to purchase a new car when she is alone and has the money to do so, she can just go out and buy one. After Jill is married to Jack, she may have to enter a long conversation about such a purchase before making it. This is a cost of marriage because the extra time spent making decisions in marriage could be allocated to some other enjoyable activity.

Economists study divorce the same way they study marriage. People choose to divorce if the expected benefits of remaining married are less than the expected costs. Another way to state this is that people divorce if the expected benefits of getting a divorce exceed the expected costs. These statements are equivalent because the benefits of remaining married are equal to the costs of divorce and the costs of remaining married are equal to the benefits of divorce.[9] The U.S. divorce rate is significantly higher than it was fifty years ago. Economists would try to explain this by looking for changes in the costs and benefits of remaining married. A higher divorce rate suggests that either the benefits of remaining married have declined or the benefits of divorce have increased, although people may have changed their preferences toward divorce.

If a person is married within a culture that stigmatizes divorce, one cost of divorce is social ostracism. Cultural acceptance of divorce increased greatly in the second half of the twentieth century, and the divorce rate increased as well because, economists would say, the cost of divorce decreased. Readers might think this is a shallow explanation of the increase in divorce because it does not address why the cultural shift occurred, but economists might respond that this question is better left to sociologists or perhaps psychologists.

Another reason for the increase in divorce is that women are more financially independent. More women in the United States are employed than they were fifty years ago. One benefit of remaining married may be continued access to the income of a spouse. A woman who is considering a divorce and who has no income of her own will find it an expensive prospect. In other words, the independent incomes of working wives may account for the increased demand for divorce. Thus a woman's having a career does not make her want to leave her husband, as some people claim, but having her own income does make it more possible for her to leave her husband if she wants to. Little has been said here about the role of husbands. Their financial independence has not changed, but now that women are less dependent on men, husbands have less financial leverage if they attempt to rule the roost, so they too are more likely to seek divorce. In other words, being able to control their wives' behavior might have been a benefit of marriage for men. Women's increasing independence has decreased this benefit and therefore may have made men more likely to divorce.

The economic model of divorce is related to an issue that might interest many social workers. A number of social workers counsel women who are victims of domestic violence. One of the most common questions is why these women choose to stay with the men who victimize them. An economist would approach this question by assuming that the costs of leaving must exceed the benefits of doing so. The economist would then try to assess the different costs and benefits that women in abusive relationships consider.

Suppose Jill is being abused by Jack and is considering leaving him. If she faces imminent poverty or the threat of murder by Jack if she leaves him, Jill may be reluctant to go, even given the abusive situation. Criminal justice and social policies that provide protection and pecuniary support to the Jills of the world could support them in their efforts to leave abusive husbands. Social workers could and perhaps should be at the forefront of efforts to get such policies enacted. Recognition of this sort of situation also raises questions about the concept of the decline of the family. A family with an abusive spouse has already declined significantly. Government policies that increase the economic costs of divorce for women in abusive relationships will probably reduce the number of divorces, but they will not lead to happier and healthier families. Thus it is hard to say that such policies would prevent the decline of the family.

The Economics of Migration

Economists also apply the rational choice model to migration. People move from one place to another if they think the benefits of moving will exceed the costs of doing so. What are some of the benefits of moving? One of the most important factors is the expectation of higher wages. The expectation of better employment opportunities also is a factor, but the available evidence shows it is not as strong a factor.[10] No doubt, other benefits enter into people's migration decisions. People may want to live closer to (or farther from) family members and friends. They may want to live in a warmer climate. They may want to live in a safer place with better schools. They may want to live someplace with more interesting cultural attractions, such as plays and museums. The list is almost endless. The fulfillment of these wants generates utility, and perhaps they should be considered in a rational choice approach to migration, but absent great relative changes in regional climate or the placement of families and cultural attractions, economists must focus on things that do undergo significant regional changes such as safety, schools, and money.

Some politicians have argued that poor people move from states with lower welfare benefits to states with higher ones. On the basis of such claims, some governors have supported two-tiered welfare systems, a bigger check for those who have lived within the state for a specific time and a smaller one for those who have lived a shorter time. These officials might be on to something. Interstate differences in welfare benefits increase the benefits of migration for recipients just as interstate differences in wages affect the benefits of migration for those in the labor market. What actually happens is not clear-cut. Some studies have found that interstate welfare benefit differences affect migration decisions at least as much as interstate wage differences, while others have found that such differences have little effect on migration.[11] Thus whether two-tiered welfare systems will have much of an effect on interstate migration is questionable.[12]

So far we have focused only on the migration decisions of potential employees and welfare recipients. Employers migrate as well, and the rational choice approach can easily be applied to these decisions. One benefit of migration that employers consider is wages; other things being equal, if wages are lower in a different region, the firm will migrate to the other region. Taxes also enter employers' calculations of the costs and benefits of moving. If a firm can lower its tax bill by migrating, it becomes more likely to do so. From a policy point of view some politicians have argued that regions that want to retain businesses would do well to enact policies to ensure that their wages and taxes are competitive with other regions.' But these politicians should never forget that competitive wages and taxes may be very low wages and taxes and therefore may be accompanied by serious suffering and destitution. Critics of the policies of trying to encourage businesses to move in (and welfare recipients to move out) call it a race to the bottom. If enough jurisdictions create competitive pressure for businesses to relocate, the tax burden will shift from the most mobile industries to those that are least able to move, and policies to make wages livable will suffer.

Some Economic Consequences of the Aging of the U.S. Population

Between 1870 and 1990 the median age of the U.S. population rose from 20.2 to 33.1 years, a rate of growth of about 1.1 years per decade.[13] Between 1990 and 2025 the median age is forecast to rise to 40.9, about 2.2 years per decade. The aging of the U.S. population is attributed to two main forces: declining fertility and increasing life expectancy. Declining fertility increases the average age of the population by reducing the number of young people relative to the number of older people.

Some analysts have projected the economic consequences of the aging of the U.S. population, such as increased costs of Social Security. The older the population, the higher the **dependency ratio,** which is a measure of the care burden placed on workers. This is the ratio of the number of Social Security recipients to workers, or

Dependency ratio = Social Security recipients ÷ Workers

For example, if the country has 20 million recipients and 100 million workers, the dependency ratio would be about 20 percent (20 million ÷ 100 million = 20 percent). That is, for everyone 1 recipient, 5 workers would be paying Social Security taxes. A lower dependency ratio means more workers are supporting each recipient, and a higher one would mean fewer workers are doing so. The dependency ratio was as low as 1 to 16 when Social Security was started in the 1930s and could go as high as 1 to 2 after the baby boom generation retires. Social Security is financed by a tax that is shared by employers and employees. Thus either taxes will have to increase or benefits will have to decrease. Neither of these options is terribly appealing.

Increasing the Social Security payroll tax is unappealing because it is a regressive tax. A tax is regressive if people with higher incomes pay a smaller percentage of their income in taxes. In 1998 employers and employees each paid 7.65 percent of wages up to a maximum of $68,400 per employee. That is, wages higher than $68,400 were not taxed for Social Security purposes. All taxpayers with a payroll income of $68,400 per year or less pay 7.65 percent of their income in taxes, but everyone with an income greater than $68,400 pays the maximum amount of payroll taxes, about $5,200 per year. This is 7.65 percent of an income of $68,400, but it is only about 3.8 percent of an income of $136,800. Thus the burden of Social Security taxes is greater for people with lower incomes than for people with higher incomes. If the government raises the Social Security tax to maintain the level of benefits in the face of a rising dependency ratio, the burden will fall more on the poor than on the rich. Perhaps the government could raise taxes on employers instead of employees. However, arguably, taxes on employers fall on workers as well if the taxes raise the cost of hiring workers. If the cost of hiring workers rises, demand for labor falls and therefore so do the wages that workers receive (see fig. 3.7). Another approach would be to increase or eliminate the $68,400 cap on taxable payroll income. Critics, however, fear that such an action will erode political support for the program.

Most readers are probably aware that Social Security is universal. That is, everyone is eligible regardless of income. Some have argued that one way to deal with the Social Security implications of the increasing dependency ratio is to make the program means tested. Under such a system only elderly people with incomes below a certain level would be eligible for the program. This proposal raises a long-standing issue that anyone who has taken a policy course in a school of social work is familiar with: Should benefits be provided to all, regardless of income, or should they just be provided to those who need the benefits most? Social workers often advocate universal programs in the belief that if everyone is a potential beneficiary, political support for the program is built in.[14] But an economist might argue that social programs should be means tested because if programs gave money only to those who need it, more funding would be available to help the poor while creating a smaller tax burden on others. An advocate of the universal approach would be likely to respond that the poor would not get more under a means-tested program because those who are not gaining from the program would resent having to pay for it.

This chapter has touched on some demographic issues that interest economists and social workers. The use of economic methodology to study these issues is still controversial, but so much of it is going on that anyone interested in policy in any of these areas should understand the economic approach. We hope that this chapter and this book have increased your understanding of how economic theory can be used to achieve a deeper examination of issues of importance to social workers.

Glossary

absolute definition of poverty: the lack of income necessary to meet basic needs

abundance: availability of a good that is greater than anyone needs or wants, or such that more of a good can be consumed without sacrificing anything else

adverse selection: exchange of a suboptimal amount caused by asymmetric information about the quality of what is being exchanged

aggregate demand: the total amount that domestic residents, businesses, government, and foreigners spend on domestically produced goods at each price level

asymmetric information: information held by one party to a transaction but not the other party

capital: physical resources used in production, such as buildings, machines, desks, paper, and the like

capitation: payment by an insurance company to service providers of a set fee based on the number of clients that providers are responsible for serving

compensation test, compensation criterion: a standard that states that a policy improves efficiency if those who gain from the policy could compensate those who lose so that, after compensation, no one would be a loser

complements: goods that are used together

cyclical unemployment (also called **demand-deficient unemployment:** unemployment caused by a decline in aggregate demand in output markets

demand: the relationship between the price and the quantity that consumers are willing to buy, all else being equal

demand-deficient unemployment: see *cyclical unemployment*

dependency ratio: the ratio of the number of Social Security recipients to workers

derived demand: demand for a particular factor or product that is dependent on the existence of a demand for some other product

discouraged workers: those who want a job but have given up looking for one and so are counted as out of the labor force

distributional weights: method of adjusting the costs and benefits of policies in order to take equity into account

efficiency (also called **Pareto efficiency**): an allocation of goods that cannot be changed to make someone better off without making at least one person worse off

efficiency-equity trade-off: the notion that policies intended to redistribute income to promote equity also curtail efficiency

elasticity of demand: see *price elasticity of demand*

elasticity of supply: see *price elasticity of supply*

equilibrium price: price at which the quantity demanded equals the quantity supplied

equilibrium quantity: a quantity that corresponds to the equilibrium price and is the point at which quantity demanded and quantity supplied are equal

external effects: see *externality*

externality (also called **external effects,** or **third-party effects**): an effect that market exchanges have on people who are not a party to those exchanges

factors of production: see *resources*

fee for service: payment by an insurance company to service providers, such as physicians, on the basis of the number of services provided

fiscal policy: the tax and spending policies of government

frictional unemployment: state at which the number of job vacancies is equal to or greater than the number of people looking for work because those seeking jobs have not been matched with those seeking workers

game theory: a branch of mathematics used by social scientists to study strategic interactions between or among firms, people, and other parties

goods: anything that at least one person finds valuable, useful, or desirable

human capital: attributes that make a worker more productive

imperfectly competitive market: any market in which the conditions of perfect competition do not obtain

income effect: a change in income that causes a change in demand for some good

inferior good: good for which demand decreases as income increases

input: see *resources*

interpersonal comparison of utility: comparison of the satisfaction that different people receive from a change in the allocation of resources

labor: the expenditure of time, effort, knowledge, and skills to produce goods in return for pay

labor market data approach: method of valuing human lives that relies on data on the trade-offs that workers make between higher and lower wages and between a higher and lower risk of death on the job

leisure: all the time spent doing anything that does not make money

lifetime earnings approach: method of valuing human life that relies on predictions of how much money a worker is likely to make during her or his lifetime

long-run economic profit: economic profit that can be sustained over the long run because new firms find that entering the market is difficult or impossible

margin: the change in some total amount caused by the last unit

marginal cost: to the consumer, the price of a good (assuming that price does not vary with the number of units purchased); to a firm, the addition to total cost caused by the last unit produced

marginal product (MP): the additional output that a company can produce by hiring one additional worker

marginal revenue: addition to total revenue caused by the last unit (if price does not vary with the number of units sold, marginal revenue equals price)

marginal revenue product (MRP): the addition to total revenue caused by the last unit added to production

marginal tax rate: the amount a person's tax bill changes for each dollar change in income

marginal utility: the additional enjoyment of the last unit

market: place where buyers and sellers come together to make exchanges

market failure: absence of one condition necessary for Pareto efficiency

market power: see *price-setting power*

mechanism design: the search for a constitution that will result in social policies that generate Pareto improvements, even though the policies are enacted and implemented only by people interested in rent seeking

monetary policy: the government's use of its influence on the money supply and interest rates

monopoly: a market with one seller and many buyers, no close substitutes for the product being sold, perfect information, and that new firms find difficult or impossible to enter

monopsony: a market that has many sellers and one buyer

moral hazard: insurance against some risk that provides an incentive to engage in behaviors that increase the likelihood that the risky event will occur

natural monopoly: a monopolistic market that exists because a single large firm can produce at lower cost than smaller firms can

nonprice competition: competition by firms that set the same price but try to win customers on grounds such as quality of service

normal good (also called **superior good**): good for which demand increases as income increases

oligopoly: a market that has a small number of sellers and many buyers, homogeneous or heterogeneous products, imperfect information, and that new firms find difficult or impossible to enter.

opportunity cost: the next best alternative forgone as a result of choosing to allocate resources in a particular way

Pareto efficiency: see *efficiency*

Pareto improvement: a change in the allocation of goods that makes at least one person better off without making anyone worse off

poverty line: amount of income needed for a person or family to purchase the amount of goods necessary for survival

poverty threshold: see *poverty line*

price elasticity of demand (also called **elasticity of demand**): a measure of the sensitivity to price of the quantity demanded; percentage change in quantity demanded for a percentage point change in price

price elasticity of supply (also called **elasticity of supply**): a measure of the sensitivity of the quantity supplied to the price; percentage change in quantity supplied for a percentage point change in price

price leadership: a market in which one firm sets the price and other firms in the industry follow

price-setting, or market, power: the ability of a single buyer or firm to influence price through its purchase or sale of a good

profit: the difference between total revenue and total cost of production

public good: a good that is available to everyone

quantity demanded: one quantity that consumers are willing to buy at a given price

quantity supplied: one quantity that suppliers are willing to sell at a given price

relative definition of poverty: possession of an income that is less than some specific portion of median income

rent avoidance: the attempt to discourage government from enacting legislation that favors a group's opponents

rent seeking: the pursuit of private profit through the political process

resources, inputs, factors of production: goods used in the production of other goods

scarcity: Insufficiency of a good for every conceivable use without sacrificing something else

statistical discrimination: discrimination based on workers' observable personal attributes because of lack of information about productivity

structural unemployment: unemployment due to insufficient demand for particular skills

substitutes: goods that can be used in place of one another

substitution effect: a change in the relative price of a good that causes a change in the quantity demanded

superior good: see *normal good*

supply: relationship between the price and the quantity that firms are willing to sell, all else being equal

third-party effects: see *externality*

total: in economics, always a running total

total cost: to the consumer, the number of units multiplied by price; to a firm, the cost of producing a given amount of output

total revenue: amount that a firm receives from all the units that it sells

total utility: subjective enjoyment that a consumer gets from all units of a good that the person has consumed thus far

unemployment: inability to find a job despite being willing and able to work and looking for a job at the going, or market, wage

utility: the subjective satisfaction of attaining one's desires

Notes

1. THE ECONOMIC PERSPECTIVE

1. As many social workers are probably aware, sociology also studies cultures, so the overlap between sociology and cultural anthropology is significant.

2. Lionel Robbins, *The Nature and Significance of Economic Science* (London: Macmillan, 1937). The contemporary definition of economics is essentially unchanged.

3. Capital, which might also be called physical capital to distinguish it from human capital, results from past investments of time and other resources.

4. Economists define *leisure* as the time spent not working for money. They consider leisure to be a type of good (see chapter 8).

5. Ben W. Lewis, *Economic Understanding: Why and What* (New York: Joint Council on Economic Education, 1957).

6. Many firms that employ social workers are nonprofits, which do not have owners but do have trustees. Although some economists study nonprofit firms, most of the discussion about companies in economic theory is about for-profit ones. This book also focuses mainly on for-profit companies. Although these are not the types of institutions that most social workers inhabit, the activities of these businesses greatly affect the well-being of social workers and their clients, as readers will see. Readers interested in the economics of nonprofits should see Burton Weisbrod, *The Nonprofit Economy* (Boston: Harvard University Press, 1988).

7. Adam Smith, *An Inquiry into the Nature and Causes of the Wealth of Nations* (1776; reprint, Oxford, U.K.: Clarendon, 1976), pp. 26–27.

8. Gary. S. Becker, *A Treatise on the Family* (Boston: Harvard University Press, 1981).

9. Peter Singer, *A Companion to Ethics* (Boston: Blackwell, 1994).

3. PERFECT COMPETITION AND THE SUPPLY-AND-DEMAND MODEL

1. Adam Smith, *An Inquiry into the Nature and Causes of the Wealth of Nations* (1776; reprint, Oxford: Clarendon, 1976).

2. Anthony B. Atkinson and Joseph E. Stiglitz, *Lectures on Public Economics* (New York: McGraw-Hill, 1980).

3. Named for the late economist-sociologist Vilfredo Pareto, who defined the conditions for efficiency.

4. Some readers may notice the similarity between figures 3.3 and 3.8. This is no accident because, except for the titles, the figures are identical. This is because we're using figure 3.8 to show what happens when government policy prevents the market from "moving" to the equilibrium price and quantity (which we discussed in reference to figure 3.3).

4. IMPERFECT COMPETITION

1. Joseph E. Stiglitz, *Economics of the Public Sector* (New York: Norton, 1988).

2. W. Kip Viscusi, John M. Vernon, and Joseph E. Harrington, *Economics of Regulation and Antitrust* (Washington, D.C.: Heath, 1992).

3. See the chapter on game theory in Shaun Hargreaves Heap et al., *The Theory of Choice: A Critical Guide* (Boston: Blackwell, 1998).

5. MARKET FAILURE AND GOVERNMENT INTERVENTION

1. Anthony B. Atkinson and Joseph E. Stiglitz, *Lectures on Public Economics* (New York: McGraw-Hill, 1980).

2. Transfers are government payments to residents for which government receives no goods in return. Welfare benefits are examples of transfers.

3. Atkinson and Stiglitz, *Lectures on Public Economics.*

4. David L. Weimer and Aidan R. Vining, *Policy Analysis: Concepts and Practice* (Englewood Cliffs, N.J.: Prentice Hall, 1992).

5. Robert W. Hahn, "Driving and Talking Do Mix." *New York Times*, November 1999, p. A33.

6. Coleman died in 1995.

7. James S. Coleman, *Foundations of Social Theory* (Boston: Harvard University Press, 1990); Gareth D. Myles, *Public Economics* (New York: Cambridge University Press, 1995); Walter Nicholson, *Microeconomic Theory: Basic Principles and Extensions* (Chicago: Dryden, 1989); Joseph E. Stiglitz, *Economics of the Public Sector* (New York: Norton, 1988).

8. Coleman, *Foundations of Social Theory*.

9. Weimer and Vining, *Policy Analysis*.

10. Michael Tanner, *The End of Welfare: Fighting Poverty in the Civil Society* (Washington, D.C.: Cato Institute, 1996).

11. George Akerlof, "The Market for Lemons," *Quarterly Journal of Economics* 84, no. 3 (August 1970): 488–500. Also see Hal R. Varian, *Intermediate Microeconomics: A Modern Approach* (New York: Norton, 1999).

12. Nicholas Barr, *The Economics of the Welfare State* (Palo Alto, Calif.: Stanford University Press, 1993). We define moral hazard in terms of insurance because the problem is thought to be especially associated with insurance markets. The problem can occur outside insurance markets, however.

6. COST-BENEFIT AND COST-EFFECTIVENESS ANALYSIS

1. Often the net benefits of a policy occur over a number of years. Economists have tools to deal with such situations, but they are beyond the scope of this book.

2. For example, the U.S. Bureau of Labor Statistics collects such data.

3. John M. Levy, *Essential Microeconomics for Public Policy Analysis* (New York: Praeger, 1995).

4. David L. Weimer and Aidan R. Vining, *Policy Analysis: Concepts and Practice* (Englewood Cliffs, N.J.: Prentice Hall, 1992).

5. Assume for the purpose of illustration that reducing teenage drinking would not also reduce domestic violence.

6. Steven Kelman, "Cost-Benefit Analysis: An Ethical Critique," in John Martin Gillroy and Maurice Wade, eds., *The Moral Dimensions of Policy Choice: Beyond the Market Paradigm* (Pittsburgh, Pa.: University of Pittsburgh Press, 1992).

7. Dorothy P. Rice and Barbara S. Cooper, "The Economic Value of Human Life," in Steven E. Rhoads, ed., *Valuing Life: Public Policy Dilemmas* (Boulder, Colo.: Westview, 1980).

8. Michael F. Drummond, Bernie O'Brien, Greg L. Stoddart, and George W. Torrance, *Methods for the Economic Evaluation of Health Care Programmes* (New York: Oxford University Press, 1999).

7. GOVERNMENT FAILURE

1. Viewing government as a benign entity was largely the approach taken by economists in the first half of the twentieth century, beginning with the early twentieth-century economist A. C. Pigou, who popularized the notion of market failure (Pigou, *Economics of Welfare* [New York: Macmillan, 1938]).

2. For an accessible discussion of the types of inefficiencies associated with government decisions, see David L. Weimer and Aidan R. Vining, *Policy Analysis: Concepts and Practice* (Englewood Cliffs, N.J.: Prentice Hall, 1992). For more in-depth works in the field see Anthony Downs, *An Economic Theory of Democracy* (New York: Harper, 1957), and James M. Buchanan and Gordon Tullock, *The Calculus of Consent* (Ann Arbor: University of Michigan Press, 1962).

3. See Gordon Tullock, "Rent Seeking," in John Eatwell, Murray Milgate, and Peter Newman, eds., *The World of Economics* (New York: Norton, 1991).

8. THE ECONOMICS OF LABOR

1. Marilyn Waring, *If Women Counted: A New Feminist Economics* (San Francisco: Harper, 1988).

2. For accessible reviews of these findings see David G. Davies, *United States: Taxes and Tax Policy* (New York: Cambridge University Press, 1986), and Gary Burtless and Barry Bosworth, "Effects of Tax Reform on Labor Supply, Investment, and Saving," *Journal of Economic Perspectives* 6, no. 1 (winter 1992): 3–25.

3. For an attempt to incorporate these more sociological considerations into an economic model of the work decision, see Chris de Neubourg, "Job Libido and the Culture of Unemployment: An Essay in Sociological Economics," in Richard Coughlin, ed., *Morality, Rationality, and Efficiency: New Perspectives on Socioeconomics* (New York: Sharpe, 1991).

4. The standard approach to modeling the demand for labor focuses on for-profit firms instead of nonprofits, which of course are the types frequented by social workers.

5. Peter K. Gottschalk, "Inequality, Income Growth, and Mobility: The Basic Facts," *Journal of Economic Perspectives* 11, no. 2 (spring 1997): 21–40.

6. See Gary S. Becker, *Human Capital: A Theoretical and Empirical Analysis with Special Reference to Education* (Chicago: University of Chicago Press, 1993).

Also see Jacob Mincer, *Schooling, Experience, and Earnings* (New York: National Bureau of Economic Research, 1974).

7. Yanis Varoufakis, *Foundations of Economics: A Beginner's Guide* (New York: Routledge, 1998).

8. Frances Fox Piven and Richard A. Cloward are two political analysts who have made this point in works that social workers are probably familiar with. See Piven, "The Historical Sources of the Contemporary Relief Debate," and Cloward, "The Contemporary Relief Debate," both in Fred Block, Richard A. Cloward, Barbara Ehrenreich, and Frances Fox Piven, *The Mean Season: The Attack on the Welfare State* (New York: Pantheon, 1987).

9. National Association of Social Workers, *Code of Ethics* (Washington, D.C.: NASW, 1996), 27.

10. Gary. S. Becker, *The Economics of Discrimination* (Chicago: University of Chicago Press, 1957).

11. William A. Darity and Patrick Mason, "Evidence on Discrimination in Employment: Codes of Color, Codes of Gender," *Journal of Economic Perspectives* 12, no. 2 (spring 1998): 63–90.

12. Richard Edwards, *Contested Terrain: The Transformation of the Workplace in the Twentieth Century* (New York: Basic, 1979); Michael Reich, "The Economics of Racism," in David B. Grusky, ed., *Social Stratification in Sociological Perspective* (Boulder, Colo.: Westview, 1994).

13. William Julius Wilson, *When Work Disappears: The World of the New Urban Poor* (New York: Vintage, 1996).

14. However, the surveys the government uses to estimate unemployment would probably count this person as unemployed.

15. Interested readers should consult a macroeconomics textbook.

16. Ronald G. Ehrenberg and Robert S. Smith, *Modern Labor Economics: Theory and Public Policy* (New York: HarperCollins, 1994).

17. The price level is a measure of overall prices in the economy.

18. Seymour S. Bellin and S. M. Miller, "The Split Society," in Kai Erikson and Steven Peter Vallas, eds., *The Sociology of Work: Sociological Perspectives* (New Haven, Conn.: Yale University Press, 1990).

19. Joel F. Handler and Yeheskel Hasenfeld, *We the Poor People: Work, Poverty, and Welfare* (New Haven, Conn.: Yale University Press, 1997).

20. Those who are currently laid off but expecting recall also are considered unemployed. Noninstitutionalized civilians who are working outside the home for pay or profit, as unpaid workers in a family enterprise, or who are temporarily absent from work for noneconomic reasons (illness, weather conditions, vacation, labor-management dispute, etc.) are considered employed. All other noninstitutionalized civilians are considered to be out of the labor force. See U.S.

Census Bureau, *Statistical Abstract of the United States* (Washington, D.C.: Hoover Business Press, 2000).

21. For further discussion of variation in unemployment rates, see Diana M. DiNitto, *Social Welfare: Politics and Public Policy* (Boston: Allyn and Bacon, 1995).

22. Bruce Meyer, "Lessons from the U.S. Unemployment Insurance Experiments," *Journal of Economic Literature* 33, no. 1 (March 1995): 91–131.

23. Lawrence Mead, *Beyond Entitlement: The Limits of Benevolence* (New York: Free Press, 1988).

24. Frances Fox Piven and Richard A. Cloward, *Regulating the Poor* (New York: Vintage, 1993).

25. The topic of inflation is beyond the scope of this book; please consult a macroeconomics textbook.

26. John Maynard Keynes, *The General Theory of Employment, Interest, and Money* (New York: Harcourt, Brace, 1935); Greg Davidson and Paul Davidson, *Economics for a Civilized Society* (New York: Norton, 1988).

27. *Keynesian* economists tend to believe that monetary and fiscal policy can be effective in reducing unemployment, but *monetarists* tend to believe that these policies are ineffective and will lead only to inflation. A detailed discussion of this debate is beyond the scope of this text. Those interested in such a discussion may wish to consult Rudiger Dornbusch and Stanley Fischer, *Macroeconomics* (New York: McGraw-Hill, 1981).

9. THE ECONOMICS OF POVERTY

1. National Research Council, *Measuring Poverty: A New Approach* (Washington, D.C.: National Academy Press, 1995).

2. Lee Rainwater, *What Money Buys: Inequality and the Social Meaning of Income* (New York: Basic, 1974).

3. John E. Schwarz and Thomas J. Volgy, *The Forgotten Americans* (New York: Norton, 1992).

4. For the 1999 official poverty line or threshold, see U.S. Census Bureau website, "Poverty Thresholds, 1999," September 26, 2000, http://www.census.gov/hhes/poverty/poverty99/pv99thrs.html (June 14, 2001); for the number of U.S. residents and percentage of the U.S. population living in poverty, see the Census Bureau website, "Poverty 1999," September 20, 2000, http://www.census.gov/hhes/poverty/poverty99/table6.html (June 14, 2001).

5. For additional criticism see National Research Council, *Measuring Poverty*.

6. Schwarz and Volgy, *Forgotten Americans*.

7. Frank Levy, *Dollars and Dreams* (New York: Russell Sage Foundation, 1987).

8. U.S. Census Bureau website, "Table 2: Poverty Status of People by Family Relationship, Race, and Hispanic Origin: 1959 to 1999," November 8, 2000, http://www.census.gov/income/histpov/hstpov02.txt (June 14, 2001).

9. Philip Harvey, *Securing the Right to Full Employment: Social Welfare Policy and the Unemployed in the United States* (Princeton, N.J.: Princeton University Press, 1989).

10. Many institutionalist and post-Keynesian economists and some others have endorsed the market power explanation.

11. A. B. Atkinson, *The Economics of Inequality* (New York: Oxford University Press, 1983).

12. Sheldon Danziger and Peter Gottschalk, *America Unequal* (Boston: Harvard University Press, 1995).

13. By "initial distribution of goods" we mean the distribution that exists before market transactions take place. If society thinks this initial distribution is unjust, it could tax those with lots of property and redistribute this revenue to those with less property. Market transactions that occur after this redistribution would result in an efficient allocation of goods and services. If this initial distribution had been redistributed in some other fashion, another efficient allocation would have resulted from market exchanges. This is what we mean in the text when we say that "there is not one efficient outcome but a different efficient outcome for every initial distribution of property." We are simplifying things quite a bit here. Those who want a slightly more advanced discussion should see Hal R. Varian, *Intermediate Microeconomics: A Modern Approach* (New York: Norton, 1999).

14. The term *Keynesian* as used here encompasses a number of distinct schools of thought, including post-Keynesians and New Keynesians, all of whom trace their origin to John Maynard Keynes.

15. The many subgroups within the neoclassical tradition are sometimes called monetarism, new classical economics, supply-side economics and the rational expectations school. All are united by, among other things, the idea that overstimulating the economy is dangerous.

16. Unfortunately, an adequate discussion of inflation is beyond the scope of this book. Those interested in an accessible discussion of this debate should consult James K. Galbraith and William Darity Jr., *Macroeconomics* (Princeton, N.J.: Houghton Mifflin, 1994).

17. For more on this topic see Galbraith and Darity, *Macroeconomics*.

18. Center on Social Welfare Policy and Law, *Implementation of the Temporary Assistance for Needy Families Block Grant: An Overview* (New York: Center on Social Welfare Policy and Law, 1996).

19. The kinds of workfare policies in TANF are not new but were parts of ear-

lier reforms. The main difference is that TANF requires more extensive participation of recipients in workfare than earlier reforms. Some evidence suggests
that former participants in earlier workfare programs who obtained jobs tended
to receive subpoverty-level wages. See Daniel Friedlander and Gary Burtless,
Five Years After (New York: Russell Sage Foundation, 1995); and Judith Guron
and Edward Pauly, *From Welfare to Work* (New York: Russell Sage Foundation,
1991).

20. Elliot Currie, *Confronting Crime* (New York: Pantheon, 1985).

21. Marlene Kim, "The Working Poor: Lousy Jobs or Lazy Workers?" Jerome
Levy Economics Institute Working Paper No. 194, May 1997, Annandale-on-
Hudson, N.Y.

22. For an example of a study that finds a link between the minimum wage
and unemployment, see Charles Brown, "Minimum Wage Laws: Are They Over-
rated?" *Journal of Economic Perspectives* 2, no. 3 (summer 1988): 133–45. For an
example of a study that shows evidence that the minimum wage does not cause
unemployment, see David Card and Alan Krueger, *Myth and Measurement: The
New Economics of the Minimum Wage* (Princeton, N.J.: Princeton University
Press, 1995).

23. Iris J. Law and Edward B. Lazere, *A Hand Up: How the Earned Income
Credits Help Working Families Escape Poverty* (Washington, D.C.: Center on Budget and Policy Priorities, 1996).

24. Ibid.

25. Harvey, *Securing the Right to Full Employment*.

26. Hyman Minsky, *Stabilizing an Unstable Economy* (New Haven, Conn.:
Yale University Press, 1986).

27. It could not, however, eliminate underemployment, as defined in chapter
8.

28. Economists also refer to this as a marginal tax rate because a benefit
reduction for each dollar increase in earnings is, in effect, a tax on the recipient's
income.

29. Gary Burtless, "The Work Responses to a Guaranteed Income: A Survey
of the Experimental Evidence," in Alicia H. Munnel, comp., Lessons from the
Income Maintenance Experiments: Proceedings of a Conference Held at Melvin
Village, New Hampshire, September 1986.

10. THE ECONOMICS OF HEALTH CARE

1. Candyce S. Berger, "Managed Care: Evolution or Revolution?" *Continuum*
(May–June 1999): 10–13.

2. U.S. Department of Commerce and U.S. Bureau of the Census, *Statistical Abstract of the United States* (Texas: Hoover's Business Press, 1998).

3. This section relies heavily on Mrigen Bose, "Organ Transplantation: Problems and Prospects," *Proceedings of the Pennsylvania Economic Association 1998 Conference*, pp. 157–68.

4. For a work by an economist who does consider what might be called the cultural effects of markets, see Samuel Bowles, "Endogenous Preferences: The Cultural Consequences of Markets and Other Economic Institutions," *Journal of Economic Literature* 36, no. 1 (March 1998): 75–111.

11. ECONOMIC DEMOGRAPHY

1. Gary S. Becker, *A Treatise on the Family* (Boston: Harvard University Press, 1981).

2. Ibid.

3. Other factors in considering cost might be the pain and suffering of childbirth.

4. *Labor,* or *work,* is used here in the economic sense of being paid by someone else to do something. Some readers may be more comfortable with the terms *paid work* or *paid labor.*

5. See Andrew Isserman, "Forecasting Birth and Migration Rates: The Theoretical Foundation," in Andrew Isserman, ed., *Population, Change, and the Economy: Social Science Theories and Models* (Higham, Mass.: Kluer Academic, 1986). Also see Glen C. Cain and Martin D. Dooley, "Estimation of a Model of Labor Supply, Fertility, and Wages of Married Women," *Journal of Political Economy* 84, no. 4 (August 1976): pt. 2, S179–99.

6. William L. Davis, Kent W. Olson, and Larkin Warner, "An Economic Analysis of Teenage Fertility," *American Journal of Economics and Sociology* 52, no. 1 (January 1993): 86–99.

7. Daniel T. Litchter, Diane K. McLaughlin, and David C. Ribar, "Welfare and the Rise in Female-Headed Families," *American Journal of Sociology* 103, no. 1 (July 1997): 112–43; Robert W. Fairlie and Rebecca A. London, "The Effect of Incremental Benefit Levels on Births to AFDC Recipients," *Journal of Policy Analysis and Management* 16, no. 4 (fall 1997): 575–97.

8. Despite considerable current discussion of a marriage penalty, a question of whether, on balance, the tax code favors or penalizes married couples remains.

9. See the discussion of opportunity cost in chapter 1.

10. Ronald G. Ehrenberg and Robert S. Smith, *Modern Labor Economics: Theory and Public Policy* (New York: HarperCollins, 1994).

11. See Paul E. Peterson and Mark C. Rom, *Welfare Magnets: A New Case for National Standard* (Washington, D.C.: Brookings Institution, 1990). Also see Thomas Vartanian, Sanford Schram, Jim Baumohl, and Joe Soss, "Already Hit Bottom: General Assistance, Welfare Retrenchment, and Single Male Migration," *Journal of Sociology and Social Welfare* 26, no. 2 (June 1999): 151–74.

12. Such systems have also been found unconstitutional, but this has not discouraged other states from trying to enact them.

13. This section draws heavily on David N. Weil, "The Economics of Population Aging," in Mark R. Rosenberg and Oded Stark, eds., *Handbook of Population and Family Economics,* vol. B (New York: Elsevier Science, 1997).

14. See Joel Blau, *Illusions of Prosperity: America's Working Families in an Age of Economic Insecurity* (New York: Oxford University Press, 1999).

Index